AGEING REWIRED

AGEING REWIRED

How to flourish in later life

LYNNE DORLING

Matador
Unit E2 Airfield Business Park,
Harrison Road, Market Harborough,
Leicestershire. LE16 7UL
Tel: 0116 2792299
Email: books@troubador.co.uk
Web: www.troubador.co.uk/matador
Twitter: @matadorbooks

ISBN 978 1803131 962

British Library Cataloguing in Publication Data.
A catalogue record for this book is available from the British Library.

Printed and bound in the UK by TJ Books LTD, Padstow, Cornwall
Typeset in 11pt Minion Pro by Troubador Publishing Ltd, Leicester, UK

Matador is an imprint of Troubador Publishing Ltd

To my daughters, Vicki and Joanna
– for adding a whole new dimension
to my 'ikigai'. Love always.

Contents

Introduction

This book has emerged from my ongoing studies in positive psychology. As part of my diploma in positive psychology and well-being, I was challenged to articulate my life purpose, which took some soul-searching. I also became increasingly interested in the topic of 'positive ageing' – a term which seems to contrast sharply with much of the writing on the experience of growing older.

I was fascinated by some of the research available and also began to notice that several of my role models in their seventies and eighties shared common characteristics. One of the main things they had in common was that they weren't afraid to 'be their own person' and genuinely appeared to feel comfortable in their own skins. They also had a sense of joie de vivre and still saw their lives as meaningful. I dug a little deeper, ran some focus groups, interviewed people and read widely to support my findings.

Ageing Rewired: How to flourish in later life is the result of that work.

Despite a steady stream of negativity in the press and alarming health statistics, we are much better informed, and I believe there has never been a more exciting time to grow old. We are to a large extent more in control of our ageing process than we might imagine, and we need all the information we can find to support ageing more positively.

Many books have been written on the benefits of having a healthy diet and lifestyle and this of course is the foundation for living a long and active life.

There are also several books around that challenge the stereotypes of old age and cite inspirational 'super agers' who fly in the face of these stereotypes.

I have read and enjoyed many of these and some are listed at the end of this book.

So, I do not cover the physical aspects of positive ageing but instead highlight some of the common characteristics of those who age well, which I have noted both from my own research and that of others.

What has been both encouraging and enlightening for me is how many of these traits can be cultivated or learned, which means there are things we can actively influence about how we age. Ideally, this book should be used as a practical aid to mental and emotional well-being. So, just as you might go for a daily walk or down your vitamins, dip in and explore this book for 'rewiring' some of the negative beliefs about ageing.

How this book works

Each chapter outlines one of the character traits of super agers that I have identified from my research. It will offer a definition, why it is important and what happens when we don't have that particular quality.

There will also be stories and examples of people who epitomise each character trait, which I hope will provide inspiration and encouragement.

Every chapter will end with a summary of key learnings and some activities that might help enhance each characteristic. The exciting thing is that any of us willing to invest time in building new habits can develop this secret armoury using the tips and techniques in this book. It is intended as a self-help guide so that you can take active steps to influence your own ageing process.

Whilst there are connections between some of the traits, each chapter stands alone and so if one or two spark your interest, start with those and come back to the others if they feel relevant.

The final section will pull together all the chapters in the form of a questionnaire and suggest ways you can create an ongoing personal action plan to embed new behaviours. There is a References and Resources section at the back of the book, which lists some further information about sources used in each chapter and a reading list for those who want to dig a little deeper.

Now in my late sixties, I had a very personal motive for researching this topic. It also gave extra meaning to my work – in my coaching practice I help people address challenges by accessing their 'best self' and playing to their strengths. So, let's work together to approach the challenges and opportunities of our 'third act' and make the most of our extra years by taking advantage of all our resources.

This is your book and one which I hope will be a useful self-help guide on how you can flourish in later life. Enjoy!

One

Sense of Purpose (*ikigai*)

'He/she who has a *why* to live for can bear almost any how.'
– Friedrich Nietzsche

What is *ikigai*?

My friend Joan, aged eighty-six, gets up each morning to unlock the church hall. She also still teaches Spanish. She walks with a stick and her eyesight is failing but she keeps an open house to provide support and a listening ear for those who need it. She is one of my personal role models and we enjoy occasional outings together for lunch and topping up our wardrobes.

Lynn, my yoga teacher, is eighty and still teaches six yoga classes a week. She is often in pain but her commitment to helping us to improve our practice is her raison d'être and her eagle eye misses nothing. She often looks after her grandchildren and a recent foot operation did not slow her down too much as she borrowed a mobility scooter and sat down to instruct her yoga class.

Dames Judi Dench and Maggie Smith continue to excel in their field and play starring roles in their eighties. Just watch how they deal with questions about ageing in the fascinating programme *Nothing Like a Dame*. I was amused to read that Dame Judi Dench had a small tattoo saying 'carpe diem' on her eightieth birthday.

John is in his mid-seventies. He is fitter than many people I know in their forties. He recently gained a qualification in sailing, is a flying instructor and still lectures on Education for Sustainability courses. He likes to set himself a new challenge every year and last summer undertook a fundraising canoe trip from Leeds to Liverpool. He has had at least four different careers, always looking for something where he can keep learning and also make a difference. I use him as an example when corporate coaching clients feel 'too old to change at fifty'.

Harry is eighty-five, a cheerful and kind man who grows vegetables and visits his wife daily who is in a care home. He worked in a wash leather factory for fifty years retiring at sixty-five to pursue his passion for gardening. When this turned into paid work, he couldn't believe his luck. He told me he had no regrets in life and feels his new *ikigai* is to lift the spirits of all he comes into contact with. As you can imagine he is a popular visitor in the care home.

Each of these people has a sense of purpose which gets them out of bed in the morning and keeps them alive.

The Japanese have a great word for this – *ikigai* – which, roughly translated, means doing what you love, what you are good at and what the world needs. Being paid for this seems to be an optional extra, which is more important to some than others, although feeling rewarded is possibly a stronger motivator.

It is well known that Japan, in particular the island of Okinawa, is at the top of the league tables for longevity. It is one of the five famous Blue Zones of the world, where more people than average live to a hundred and beyond. The other four are Sardinia in Italy, Loma Linda in California, The Nicoya Peninsula in Costa Rica and Ikaria, an isolated Greek island. I was fortunate enough to visit Japan and stay in Ishigaki (part of the Okinawa Prefecture) a few years ago and was immediately struck by the sense of calm everywhere. Even at busy times in the restaurant at the beautiful resort we stayed in, the staff were patient, and the service was excellent. One night, the head chef noticed us puzzling over some of the Japanese dishes and took us through the whole range of options on the extensive menu, telling us with pride what ingredients had gone into them. We were literally spoilt for choice, and I was impressed by the passion and purpose he clearly got from his work. Apart from their healthy diet, there are other lessons we can learn from Japanese culture – more of that later.

I would highly recommend reading Hector Garcia and Francesc Miralles' engaging book called *Ikigai*, detailing the findings of their year-long research into the Japanese lifestyle, with words of wisdom from centenarians and beyond.

My story

So, what is your 'sense of purpose'? This is a big question and one that I've been tussling with for years. Whilst I love my work as a coach, I've increasingly been reflecting on how meaningful my contribution is and what legacy I will leave. This was especially highlighted as much of this writing was completed when we were in lockdown during the 2020 Covid-19 pandemic. I noticed even more what 'lit my eyes up' and what felt worthwhile. Writing, on topics I feel passionate about, was one of these things. Combining both my passions of coaching and writing, I started to see myself as a catalyst with the potential to inspire others to take action.

When you consider something as all-encompassing as purpose it is tempting to think this must be something monumental like trying to change the education system or reducing the stigma around mental health.

A good question to ask yourself is what makes you angry and what might you feel strongly enough to act on, even in a small way?

Then consider what you might already be doing, using your strengths and day-to-day opportunities to work towards that aim.

Let me use an example.

Three years ago, I took a sabbatical to complete a diploma in positive psychology and wellbeing (DPP) with the Langley Group. This was one of the best programmes I have been involved in – not only pulling together much of my previous learning but raising my awareness of my strengths and individual talents. We were encouraged to choose two areas of particular interest to focus on for additional studies. Answering my own questions about what I felt strongly about, I chose positive mental health and positive ageing.

Whilst both of these felt like huge 'causes', I would like to think that by writing this book on how to age more positively, and integrating some of my learning into my coaching practice, I am using my talents and experience to make a small difference in these areas. Martin Seligman, who is usually credited with being the founder of positive psychology, describes it as a 'buffer against mental illness'.

In my coaching practice, I have always tried to work with what people do well and what they can do more of rather than try and 'fix' them. This is the whole philosophy on which Martin Seligman founded positive psychology as a separate discipline almost twenty years ago. On my DPP, I was heartened to learn the neuroscience behind this and the positive impact on health and well-being of 'playing to our strengths'. As part of the programme, we completed a strengths profile, which measured not only how good we were at things but how often we used these strengths and how energised we were by them. It was a revelation to me to note so many unrealised strengths, almost 'hidden talents', which I was not using very often. I also noted strengths I was overusing and which maybe didn't energise me so much anymore. I am fortunate that I run my own business so was able to act on the results and let go of some of the things I was good at but which no longer energised me or gave me job satisfaction.

What a dramatic effect this had on my motivation and energy levels. Noticing what you love and what you are good at is a huge part of *ikigai*. I have also been able to apply this to some of my coaching clients to encourage better delegation and application of their own underused strengths.

My work now has a new sense of purpose – working with others and helping them play to their strengths has reignited my passion for coaching. As for 'what the world needs', I have actively sought out like-minded people who share my beliefs and passion for spreading 'positive ripples'. My cohort from the DPP formed an alumni group, and we are ambassadors for the benefits that positive psychology has to offer. I became more selective with my corporate clients, partnering with those who took health and well-being seriously. I actively volunteered in new sectors, such as a local secondary school, which made very good use of my enthusiasm and resources for positive psychology. This gave me a great sense of 'giving back' and doing something worthwhile. I've aligned myself with organisations who are focused on the bigger picture and making a positive difference in the world. I am proud to be an ambassador and active member of Action for Happiness, a fantastic charity whose mission is 'to increase positivity and reduce negativity in the world' – their patron is the Dalai Lama, and the charity is run by an inspirational leader, Mark Williamson. I also believe that this community offers people a sense of belonging to a greater cause and a chance to learn some techniques to improve their mental well-being. Their Action for Happiness app is free to download and provides a couple of positive boosts to me daily.

Finally, I'd like to share a very personal story, which brought home to me how vital it is to find meaning in our activities.

It was day four of the DPP. It had been a brilliant, intense and emotional few days. We were given a group task to build a complicated model. Even with detailed instructions, I was struggling. So were my colleagues. What was the point of this? We were frustrated and more focused on our coffee break than the task in hand. Then we had a break, and afterwards, our leader showed us a video clip. We were initially unsure of the relevance. It showed adults and children from different parts of the world with missing limbs writing and drawing using prosthetic hands. They were smiling, happy and grateful. And that is what we were making: prosthetic hands for a small but wonderful charity called Helping Hands. There wasn't a dry eye in the room. I guess it also had a deeper personal meaning to me, as my nephew was born with only part of his left arm and has become so dextrous with his prosthetic limb that he now paints beautiful tiny model figures and is a whizz at DIY!

After the video we immediately got on with our task, redoubling our efforts and totally engaged now we understood the bigger picture and had a sense of purpose and meaning to our work.

Leaders of the world take note!

What happens if you don't have *ikigai*?

Many years ago, when I worked in corporate life, I was privileged to have a short-term role as a manager for a team of internal coaches who provided outplacement support following a big restructure.

Many of those who were made redundant had seen themselves as 'lifers' and were devastated to go. Whilst the financial packages were generous, none of this fully compensated for a sudden lack of meaning which they had got from their work and our team had to use all their skills to help people rebuild purposeful lives. There was learning for many of us doing this work too: not to put all our eggs in one basket. In other words, have a healthy 'whole life' rather than expecting all your life satisfaction and purpose to come from one area, whether that is work or a key relationship. There is a useful activity in appendix 1 for you to review your own life balance. (Also see chapter six on perspective for another aspect of this case study.)

In a less dramatic but no less painful way, 'empty nesters' feel a distinct lack of purpose when children leave home. This often leads to inappropriate hanging on to children, which can hinder their own growing up process.

Whilst few of us would want to go to the extremes of parenting that Richard Branson's mother did – leaving him to find his own way home from the countryside when he was just five years old – many of us need to consider whose needs we are fulfilling when we are still providing washing/ironing/cleaning services for our twenty-somethings!

Not surprisingly, some people feel totally lost when they lose a life partner or have to go into a care home. There is now much more awareness of how even small things like caring for a house plant or choosing when and what to have for lunch can make them feel more in control and improve their general well-being. Experiments were conducted on this many years ago by Ellen Langer, a Harvard psychologist, and her team, and these are documented in her book *Counterclockwise*.

It is hard work to reshape your life to include new and meaningful activities after divorce, bereavement or retirement and it takes time and commitment. However, small steps can make a big difference. Arianna Huffington describes the 'new science of microsteps', which can lead to behavioural change, in her recent book *Your Time to Thrive*.

One of my favourite sights on my daily walk is a lovely lady in her nineties who lives at a local care home, picking up litter with her stick. This sense of improvement for her environment is something she really cares about and gives her an incentive for getting out there.

What does the research say?

Many people have written about a sense of meaning, *Man's Search for Meaning* by Viktor Frankl perhaps being one of the first to spring to mind. He was intrigued by how some people can survive the worst horrors imaginable whilst others just give up.

One of the many things that resonated with me from his book was that everything can be taken away from a person except one thing: their choice of how to react in any given set of circumstances. A sense of meaning or purpose to one's life can really influence this.

For example, Frankl had the manuscripts for his book (several years of work) confiscated on arrival at Auschwitz. Whilst he had a slim chance of survival in the concentration camps, he credits the need to rewrite these manuscripts as a major factor in overcoming the odds. He often remembered the quote at the beginning of this chapter by the philosopher Friedrich Nietzsche:

'He/she who has a *why* to live for can bear almost any how.'

He also saw many people lose hope and perish but was able to find meaning in his own suffering because he saw it as a means to an end.

The aim of positive psychology is to look at what enables people to flourish and the conditions required for optimal functioning. Chris Peterson, another of the founding fathers of the discipline, described it as 'the scientific study of what makes life worth living'.

Paul Wong, an early pioneer and researcher in this field, also captured it eloquently:

'Without a personally defined meaning and purpose, individuals would describe life as being on a ship without a rudder.'

In his comprehensive work detailed in *The Human Quest for Meaning*, Wong describes his PURE Model, which represents the four elements that define meaning. See below for a simplified version adapted from this model:

P – is for Purpose. What should I do with my life?

U – is for Understanding. How do I make sense of the world?

R – is for Responsible Action. What choices should I make?

E – is for Enjoyment. Am I happy with how I am living my life?

A concept also recognised by many of these researchers is that of 'post-traumatic growth'. We can often see this in everyday life, where someone who has been diagnosed with a terminal disease suddenly finds a new lease of life by writing or fundraising to help others with their condition. Without exception, these people have talked about this providing a meaning to their suffering. (See chapter three on resilience for more on this topic.)

One of the things evidence suggests is that those who give up hope in the face of adversity can experience a decline in their mental and physical health, as observed poignantly by Viktor Frankl.

'Woe to him who saw no more sense in his life, no aim, no purpose, and therefore no point in carrying on. He was soon lost.'
– Viktor Frankl

The mind-body connection is very powerful and two of my favourite books on this topic are *Your Body Speaks Your Mind* by Deb Shapiro and *You Can Heal Your Life* by Louise Hay.

Again, a personal example brought home to me just how much the body is connected to the mind. I was going through some difficult times with my ageing parents. I suffered from regular gum infections, so much so that my dentist, who was also a very good listener, used to give me antibiotics before a holiday 'just in case'. Looking up my symptoms, problems with the teeth or gums can be connected to 'mother love' and letting go. Of course, a more logical person might just surmise that I was under additional stress and my immune system was compromised.

Another recent discovery for me has been craniosacral therapy (CST): a gentle non-invasive treatment which works with your 'inner physician' to stimulate the body's natural healing process. I found it very powerful and effective for relieving long-standing neck pain and headaches.

How does this relate to positive ageing?

There are some common threads and observations to all this research on meaning and purpose:

- Having a sense of purpose is widely believed to help 'buffer' people through difficult times by increasing hope or optimism, both of which are positive indicators for longevity (see chapter two on optimism).

- There is a growing body of evidence to support the concept that people who have a sense of purpose live longer (JAMA Network Open Study, 2019).

- There is a strong connection between meaning in life and psychological well-being. Carol Ryff developed a psychological well-being questionnaire which I found very helpful when working on my own sense of purpose.

- People who lack meaning or purpose in their lives are more susceptible to low mood or depression (Centre for Ageing Better).

Summary

So having a sense of purpose can definitely give us a raison d'être and encourage us to get out of bed each day. It keeps us motivated, which has to be a good thing as we get older. Back to the Japanese, who do not have a word for 'retirement' so keep doing what they love and are good at for as long as they can. They also have a strong sense of community, and it is increasingly believed that caring for others can provide meaning and purpose to our lives.

Let me end this chapter with a summary of key learnings and some suggestions of how to start developing a more purposeful life.

Key learnings

- Having a raison d'être has a profound positive effect on our mental and physical well-being.
- Small things can make a big difference – knowing ourselves and what is important to us can guide us in defining our purpose and life goals.
- Playing to our strengths can build positive emotions and increase motivation and engagement.
- There is a strong connection between meaning in life and psychological well-being.
- Having a sense of purpose in life can help us live longer.

Activities

Discovering our own sense of purpose

Here are four activities to help you to find or rediscover your purpose and give more meaning to your everyday life:

1) Pursue your passion

Allow some time to reflect on the following questions – this may be an activity you want to revisit several times. As outlined in this chapter, it was a gradual process which brought out my own passion for positive ageing.

- What issues or causes do you feel strongly enough about to want to change?
- How could you be part of the change even in a small way?

- What would you like to look back on in five years' time and be proud to have been a part of?
- What have you always wanted to spend more time doing 'when you have more time'?
- What skills/talents/experience do you have already that might equip you for working on this?

2) Play to your strengths

The Via Institute on Character describes strengths as the pathways to meaning. Complete their free online strengths survey to find out more about your own.

Once you have your top five strengths, ask yourself how you are living these to the full. Use them to add more meaning to your life.

3) Practise your values

Do you know what your top values are? These reflect who you are at a very deep level, your core beliefs and driving forces. Quite simply they are what you stand for in the world.

My own include the following:
- Well-being
- Personal development
- Contribution
- Creativity
- Fun

Whenever I feel 'out of sync' or demotivated, I check in to see which one of these is not being honoured. For example, my top priority is health and well-being, so I had to give myself a pep talk recently when I realised I was not 'walking my talk' in some areas.

The following questionnaire is designed for you to identify your own values:

Values Questionnaire

- Consider the list of values below.
- Identify how important they are to you.
- Tick the relevant box for each (not important, quite important, very important)
- Decide which are your 5 most important values and summarise in the box at the end of this questionnaire.

Description of value	Not important	Quite important	Very important
Belonging – participating with, being involved and including others			
Challenge – adventure, new and exciting experiences			
Compassion – caring for others and relieving suffering			
Contribution – assisting others and improving society			
Creativity – being imaginative, inventive and original			
Economic security – having steady and adequate income			
Environment – geographical location and physical surroundings			
Equality – enabling fairness and inclusive participation			
Flexibility – having freedom and choice to work in your own way			
Fun – enjoying activities and bringing humour into your daily life			
Inner harmony – congruence with who you are and what you do			
Integrity – keeping your word, standing up for your beliefs			

Description of value	Not important	Quite important	Very important
Order – organised, structured, systematic			
Personal development – continuous learning and realising your potential			
Playing to strengths – using experience, skills and expertise			
Recognition – gaining respect and acknowledgement			
Self–belief – belief in your abilities, self – respect			
Variety – enjoying a diverse range of projects			
Wellbeing – physical, mental and emotional good health			
Work–life balance – being able to spend quality time with family			
Top 5 Values 1. 2. 3. 4. 5.			

Adapted from Values Questionnaire LBD Associates Ltd

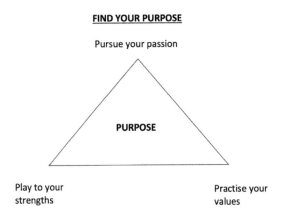

FIND YOUR PURPOSE

Pursue your passion

PURPOSE

Play to your
strengths

Practise your
values

4) Purpose Triangle

Once you have read this chapter and completed the first three activities, use the Purpose Triangle to pull all your learning together. Transfer your passion, top three strengths and top three values to the model above. This should help you clarify your purpose and what it means to you.

I have also included this model again at the back of the book in case you want to add to it/amend or refine it once you have read other chapters and completed more activities.

Two

Optimism

'A pessimist sees the difficulty in every opportunity; an optimist sees the opportunity in every difficulty.'
– Winston Churchill

What is optimism?

According to the Cambridge Dictionary, it is 'the quality of being full of hope and emphasising the good parts of a situation, or a belief that something good will happen'.

My own observations are that optimists have a positive mental attitude (PMA), a 'can do' approach and expect the best, even if they might also prepare for the worst. They practise gratitude, which is another 'muscle' that grows with daily practice (see Activities at end of this chapter). They count their blessings, however small, and often seem to have faith in something beyond themselves.

We all know people who are 'half full' or 'half empty'. What I notice most about spending time with an optimist is how energised and uplifted I come away feeling. The opposite is true if I am unfortunate enough to spend time with a born pessimist, who my friend describes as an 'energy vampire'. It is hard work trying to stay positive if you surround yourself with pessimists.

Why is optimism important?

I once had the great pleasure of hearing Dr Maria Sirois speak to a large audience at an Action for Happiness event. Her work as a clinical psychologist helping families and children facing terminal illness equipped her admirably to talk about 'Happiness in Dark Times'. She held the audience in thrall as she began with the following metaphor.

She invited us first to focus on all the things which were stressful and negative in our lives – there was no shortage of suggestions for this pile – which she nicknamed the 'swamp'. Even just talking about the issues – bad bosses, transport problems, money worries, house prices, health issues etc – dragged us down.

Then she asked us to think about all of the things that cheer us up: friends, family, sunshine, holidays, good food etc. As we shouted out suggestions, we could feel ourselves smiling. This felt much more uplifting, and she nicknamed this pile the 'pond'.

Consider this – what we focus on gets bigger. So, if we spend our time worrying and listening to all the negativity in the world, this is likely to affect our mood and we start to expect the worst. If, on the other hand, we choose to actively look for and focus on the good things, guess what? We start noticing even more of them.

This resonated with me deeply as I was beginning this chapter about optimism as I really agree that we can choose to be 'half full' or 'half empty' – not that we should all be Pollyanna types and ignore the swamp, but by focusing more on the pond, those positive ripples start to grow. Two strategies I have developed to keep myself buoyant are meditation and setting limits for time spent on social media.

> 'Remember the blue sky. It may at times be
> obscured by clouds, but it is always there.'
> – Andy Puddicombe, Headspace

Case study

My friend Sue is often in great pain. She has had serious back problems, including surgery which was not very successful. She recently lost her beloved husband who she had cared for in the latter years. It is very rare that I see her feel sorry for herself. She has made a habit of 'living life in the positive column' and is constantly thankful for all she has. She goes out of her way to help others, generously volunteers her time and is an active member of her church. She has deliberately cultivated a positive support network around her and, even when in severe pain, can usually keep life in perspective. She often tells me how fortunate she feels in her life.

Case study

My dear mum, Dorothy, was always 'half full' – in the most difficult times she expected the best and whatever happened she could turn it into a silver lining. She and my dad counted their blessings daily, and my sister and I were in no doubt just how much we were loved. Even when Dorothy got Alzheimer's in her mid-seventies, she used to say, 'well at least it's not painful'. Whilst I used to think privately that it might not be painful for her, it was very tough on the rest of the family. However, I was in awe of her ability to always remember there were people much worse off than herself.

Case study

My friend's mother is in her nineties. In the last couple of years, she has lost her husband, a daughter and another family member and now lives alone. She counts her blessings daily and has rebuilt her life with the help of family and friends. She feels lucky to live in an area of great natural beauty and has a large garden which keeps her busy and active. She also still drives which keeps her independent. She has a large and attentive family who she keeps in touch with regularly on her iPad. They see her as a true advocate for positive ageing.

What happens if we don't have optimism?

So why does optimism matter and what happens if we don't have it? Even more importantly, how does it link to positive ageing?

Well, there is a great deal of research to support the fact that those who expect the worst usually find that it can be a self-fulfilling prophecy.

'Whether you think you can, or you think you can't – you're right.'
– Henry Ford

'If we habitually believe that misfortune is our fault, is enduring and will undermine everything we do, more of it will befall us than if we believe otherwise.'
– Martin Seligman

One of my coaching clients had an important meeting coming up to discuss his return to work after a long absence. We had discussed how he might approach this to suggest adaptations to his role which were agreeable on both sides. He decided to handle things his own way and seemingly only presented a list of his own needs, without recognising the company's expectations. Afterwards he told me 'it went exactly as I expected – they just wouldn't listen and never will'.

Pessimism can negatively impact on our health, well-being and even our longevity. This is borne out by the following examples.

According to a report published by the Centre for Ageing Better, pessimism around getting older is linked to poorer health. Those who worry more and expect to feel lonely are 30% more likely to have a negative experience of ageing.

An interesting study was carried out on a group of nuns who had to write letters about what they imagined life would be like before they entered a nunnery. Many years later, their stories were studied for emotional variance and related to survival rates. Those who were positive and expected the best from their experience lived an average of seven years longer than those who were less optimistic. Quite literally, they had primed their brains to expect the best.

There is also some evidence to suggest that the dread of something may actually be worse than the experience itself.

A study done by the AARP (American Association of Retired Persons) found that 47% of respondents aged between eighteen and thirty-nine said 'it's normal to be depressed when old'.

Only 10% of the over sixties described old age as a depressing life stage. In fact, British adults report the highest level of happiness and life satisfaction after sixty.

According to The State of Ageing 2019 report, life satisfaction peaks between seventy and seventy-four. Good news for 'super agers'!

This raises an important point – can optimism be learned or are we born half full or half empty?

What does the research say?

So, let's examine optimism a little more carefully and consider whether it can be developed. Martin Seligman defines it as 'a tendency to expect the best possible outcome or dwell on the most hopeful aspects of a situation'.

I have long been fascinated by the debate about 'nature' versus 'nurture', and I was heartened by the research surrounding 'learned optimism' which leads us to believe we are more in control of this attribute than many people imagine.

Sonja Lyubomirsky wrote an interesting book called *The How of Happiness*, in which she describes the Happiness Pie. Although there is some debate around the statistics, her research suggests that only 50% of our happiness levels are genetic. Whilst we all have hereditary traits and some people are more predisposed to a negative outlook on life, we have a choice whether to act on this and we can do much to counteract it. It is likely that up to 40% of our own happiness levels are within our control.

For example, I have two friends, both of whom play a role in caring for their elderly mothers who, without being unkind, are born pessimists. What I notice is how the daughters have both chosen to be upbeat, optimistic and cheerful and do all they can to resist the negative influence of their mothers.

It would be easy to say that circumstances play a big role. Some pessimists I know also have a 'victim mentality' and say things like 'it's all right for you – you have money' or 'if it wasn't for this health issue, I could do so much more'.

On our DPP, I was surprised to find from Sonja Lyubomirsky's research how little difference life circumstances make. A survey was done on lottery winners, whose happiness levels peaked after the win but were likely to be back to their 'set point' a year later. Equally, some research on people with life-changing injuries found that after an understandable dip in their happiness levels, one year on, many were back to their initial levels of happiness (some even more so – see chapter three on resilience).

So, it is exciting to know that as much as 40% of our happiness level might be within our control. There are so many intentional daily activities we can do to keep ourselves in a good place. One thing I often do with my coaching clients is to get them to think about where they get their energy from – not only physical but also mental and social – as well as the kind of environment that makes them feel at their best. Just by brainstorming a few activities which make them feel good, and setting a daily intention to do at least two or three, can make a big difference to their mood and energy. There is an activity at the end of this chapter for you to create your own Happy List. Happiness is a choice you must make every day if you want to retrain your brain to think more positively.

In his book, *Learned Optimism*, Martin Seligman goes a step further and implies that optimism is a key criterion for success alongside aptitude and motivation. He has conducted studies to prove this in recruitment situations. The book also contains information about the explanatory styles of optimists versus pessimists – your natural thinking style and the messages you give to yourself. Once you become more aware of this, there are some useful techniques for reframing your 'self-talk' to shift your mindset. There is an activity at the end of chapter six on perspective called 'thinking traps', along with some suggestions of how to train your brain to think differently. It is perfectly possible to 'rewire' the brain and create new neural pathways which make new ways of thinking more automatic.

> 'For the brain to rewire itself, it requires sustained practice of a new behaviour, which will sufficiently challenge the brain to think in a new way.'
> – Tara Stewart

Gratitude

A daily practice which has had an extraordinary impact on my own intention to become a 'realistic optimist' is gratitude.

On our DPP course we were encouraged to start thinking of three things daily which had gone well and then at least five things for which we were grateful. At first, I found this quite difficult, and a bit contrived, but persevered. I now do this every evening and can regularly list at least ten things I am grateful for, see below for examples.

The accumulative impact of this daily practice has had a marked effect on my levels of optimism. I now actively look for the good

Gratitude list

What's gone well today?	What am I grateful for?
• Completed my first chapter • Did a hard personal training session • Met up with a friend for coffee	• A lovely sunny day • My husband's support with the book • An uplifting film • Flowers from the garden • A new book • A good night's sleep • Knowing my daughters are safe • A mug of hot chocolate • Finding a new playlist • A card from a friend

things. With the pond and the swamp in mind, even on the most difficult day it can be possible to find one good thing if you cultivate this as a habit. My daughter has a gratitude jar, which she fills with post-it notes of her daily observations. What an uplifting activity it is to dip into these on a less positive day.

Different levels of happiness

My studies on the DPP also encouraged me to explore the differences between hedonic and eudaimonic happiness.

In our society today, there is a lot of focus on 'hedonism': being happy in the moment, pleasure-seeking and immediate gratification, often fuelled by social media. Whilst this might provide short-term happiness, it can often leave a yearning for a deeper level of fulfilment, known as 'eudaimonia'. This is about finding a deeper sense of meaning and satisfaction, which often requires some soul-searching and internal growth to discover. I think we are fortunate to live in times where there are so many resources and choices available for personal development, which offer opportunities to explore this concept. Chapter one on sense of purpose is a good place to start with defining what really matters to you and what is more likely to lead to that deeper level of life satisfaction. Many people had to re-evaluate their priorities when some of the more hedonistic pleasures (e.g. eating out, socialising, going for a massage etc.) were curtailed in the lockdowns during the 2020 Covid-19 pandemic. I know of several people who made changes to their career, health regime or relationships following the pandemic.

The power of positive emotions

Barbara Lee Fredrickson is an American professor of psychology at the University of North Carolina. She has been studying emotions for more than twenty years and in particular how positive emotions such as love, joy and gratitude contribute to happiness. She found that positive emotions affect our brain differently to negative emotions. They appear to have a 'broadening effect' on our thoughts and behaviours, often increasing our ability to be creative and come up with new solutions to problems. In contrast to this, more traditional responses are often triggered by negative emotions like fear, anger and disgust. This led to her Broaden and Build Theory which suggests that by experiencing more positive emotions, we broaden our range of perspectives and actions, which builds lasting physical, intellectual and psychological resources. There is even some evidence to suggest that positive emotions may help us to minimise the impact of negative emotions. This is 'rewiring' at its best and provides a powerful incentive to actively cultivate a positive mindset.

These are persuasive arguments indeed for fostering happier families, workplaces, communities and societies. In her book *Positivity*, Barbara Fredrickson suggests that a ratio of 3:1 of positive/negative experiences is needed for optimal levels of well-being and resilience.

How does this relate to positive ageing?

Whilst many workplaces are putting employee well-being higher on their agenda, there is also an increasing need to reach the ageing population with some of this information. As we already know, pessimism in older adults leads to poorer health. Guy Robertson's book *How to Age Positively* is a great self-help resource, which includes some useful tips and techniques for cultivating a more positive outlook in later life. There are three short chapters on positive thinking which include neurolinguistic programming (NLP) techniques for replacing negative beliefs with positive ones, visualisation techniques and a good explanation of Martin Seligman's 'ABCDE strategy', which can help to challenge pessimistic thoughts and increase optimism. Ideally, this book should be worked through with a trusted confidante or coach.

I wanted to share a personal story which illustrates the benefits of getting an older person to focus on the positives.

A couple of years ago, I was privileged to be involved in an experimental intergenerational project between a primary school and local care home. As a volunteer driver, I was invited to have tea with a group of residents and children who were spending time getting to know each other. It was apparent that many of the older people had dementia, and I talked with one lady in her nineties for a while. As a coach, I had always thought I was good at asking questions but found myself struggling to find a topic of mutual interest. A young girl called Sophie joined us, and I was in awe of this nine-year-old's ability to quickly build a rapport with Daphne, who told her she had been at the care home for three years. The next question, 'and do you have fun?' brought Daphne alive and she said they had fun every day and started to tell her about the kind of activities she enjoyed: the garden, sewing, singing etc. This playful question allowed Daphne to focus on fun, not to try and recall facts that may have been long forgotten.

This incident also reminded me of trying to keep communication channels open with my own mum when she was living with dementia. There was a somewhat controversial method of relating to dementia patients called SPECAL (Specialist Early Care for Alzheimer's) being promoted at the time, which was described as 'a person-centred method of managing dementia and promoting well-being'. Carers and family members are encouraged to follow 'three golden rules':

1. Not to ask direct questions to which the patient may not know the answer.
2. To listen and learn from the expert: the person with dementia.
3. Not to contradict or correct them.

The aim of this method is to reinforce positive emotions and minimise distress and anxiety. This fitted well with my philosophy of working with the memories which are left rather than continually highlighting what is missing.

Summary

So, whatever stage of life we are in, cultivating a positive mental attitude can influence our health and well-being.

The most important thing to remember is that we can choose how to respond to circumstances. This is certainly not a new finding but one we may need reminding of from time to time:

'Each player must accept the cards life deals him or her, but once they are in hand, he or she alone must decide how to play the cards in order to win the game.'
– Voltaire

Key learnings

- What we focus on gets bigger – choose the pond, not the swamp!
- Expecting the worst can become a self-fulfilling prophecy, which can negatively impact on health, well-being and longevity.
- Up to 40% of our happiness levels may be within our control.
- Optimism can be learned or increased through intentional activities.
- Positive emotions expand our thinking capacity and build lasting physical, intellectual and psychological resources.

Activities

Developing your PMA (positive mental attitude)

Here are three suggested activities which might help you develop a more positive mindset:

1) Gratitude diary
Start a gratitude diary. Each day, make a note of three things which have gone well and up to ten things you are grateful for.

Don't worry if you can only think of one good thing or five things you appreciate at first. This is a regular daily practice well worth developing for our well-being – remember, it takes sixty-six days to embed a new habit.

Keep practising and notice what happens with your mood. You can also use this diary to check back on the good things in life when things aren't going so well.

2) Your best self

What are your strengths, talents, unique qualities? You have already started thinking of these in the last chapter. However, on a bad day, it is often difficult to remember these. What do people most value about you? Choose five or six people you know and trust (family, friends, work colleagues, clients) and ask them the following questions:

- What three words would you use to describe me?
- When do you see me at my best?
- What do you think is my number one strength?

It may be easier to send them an email, telling them you are doing this as part of your personal development. Some people find it hard to ask for feedback face to face and those you have chosen will need time to prepare.

Thank everyone for their feedback. Take time to savour the results and highlight any themes which come out of this for you.

How are you using these talents and qualities? What else

could you do? Consider how they may help you with your Purpose Triangle in the last chapter.

3) What's in your 40% bucket?[1]

Do you remember we talked about intentional lifestyle activities which can keep you feeling positive and upbeat? Use the boxes below to brainstorm all the activities you could do to keep yourself in a good place. It is divided into four quadrants: Body, Brain, Environment and Relationships. Having some activities in each segment will help you to build your physical, mental, intellectual, emotional and social resources.

What are your top strategies for keeping yourself in a good place? I have given an example in each of the boxes.

What's in your 40% bucket?

BRAIN	BODY
Learning Spanish	Yoga
ENVIRONMENT	**RELATIONSHIPS**
Lighting a candle	Volunteering

---

1   Activity reproduced with kind permission of the Langley Group.

Fill in as many as you can or work with a friend on this, and then make a commitment to do at least one thing you enjoy from each quadrant every day. Review after a month and notice the impact on your mood. See appendix 2 for more ideas for each quadrant.

Three

Resilience

'Fall down seven times, stand up eight.'
– Japanese proverb

What is resilience and how do we know when people have it?

Some people describe resilience as 'bouncing back' quickly from difficulties, whereas I prefer to think of it as 'bouncing beyond', having integrated the learning from a particularly challenging time.

Resilience is the lynchpin for many of the other characteristics defined in this book. In particular, I have noticed that resilient people learn from experience and keep going in the face of adversity. They have self-belief and apply optimistic thinking to a tough task. They have courage, backbone, determination and grit.

For example, I was recently waiting for a return flight from a very enjoyable trip to Portugal. As speedy boarders we were ushered out onto the tarmac to wait in line. There was a cool breeze, and I was glad of my jacket. We had quite a wait. Beside me, I noticed a group of four people: a middle-aged couple with several suitcases and a much older couple. The older lady was in a wheelchair and was trying to keep warm with a thin blanket. When we got chatting, it transpired that the older couple were in their nineties and they were returning from a few days in Lisbon. It had not gone according to plan.

En route, their original flight was delayed by snow and after being stuck in a freezing cold lift for over an hour, they eventually had to stay overnight and catch a flight the next day. The younger woman told me that, for her, it had taken the edge off the whole week. Then I looked at the nonagenarians, the lady calm and stoic in her wheelchair and her husband sprightly and cheerful as he sprinted across the tarmac carrying his suitcase. For them, that had been just a minor setback, which did not stop them enjoying their planned break. Whether this was resilience, grit or ability to keep life in perspective, I envied their attitude.

'Studies show that "superagers" appear to be more resilient to the slings and arrows of life.'
– *The Guardian*, February 2018

A word about 'grit'

Angela Duckworth, Professor of Psychology at the University of Pennsylvania, defines the term 'grit' as follows: 'Grit is passion and perseverance for long-term and meaningful goals.'

Read Angela Duckworth's book, entitled *GRIT – The Power of Passion and Perseverance* for more on this topic.

So, in the context of this book, resilience and determination combined with a passion or purpose seems likely to encourage people to redouble their efforts in the face of adversity.

In terms of 'super agers', I can think of no better example of someone who demonstrates resilience and grit in spades than Irene Obera, the American track and field athlete.

Case study

At the age of eighty-four, Irene was described as the fastest woman on earth for her age. Having overcome several health challenges in her early years, she pushed herself to achieve fitness goals and then broke world records in Masters Athletes for four decades. Her motto is: 'A quitter never wins and a winner never quits – I want to be a winner.'

Being a winner was the sense of purpose which drove her to come out of retirement five times and to keep up a punishing regime of training combined with bowling, tennis and gym sessions just for fun! Not surprisingly, Irene is the picture of good health and looks much younger than her years.

What happens if we don't have resilience?

Low resilience can cause physical illness, depression and

anxiety. People with low resilience can be easily overwhelmed by problems whereas resilient people find a way to deal with problems or setbacks.

We all know people who have had hard knocks in life who then just seem to give up. This can become a downwards spiral, which is much harder to reverse. Once people fall into a 'victim' mentality where they feel they have very little control, this can have a very negative impact on their state of mind. Life can appear quite meaningless, and many people cut themselves off from others.

One of the best life skills we can pass on to the next generation is how to manage their own expectations. Life will inevitably have ups and downs, and it is often from the toughest times we can learn the most. Developing skills and resources to navigate those peaks and troughs at an early age will reap benefits in later years. This was never more relevant than during the 2020 Covid-19 pandemic when so many plans were put on hold. Learning to manage emotions is a key skill worth developing.

For example, I recently coached two very different characters who had similar life experiences. Both had been bereaved, one in shocking circumstances. One chose to try and 'carry on as normal' and slid into a depressed state of mind. He was signed off work with stress.

The other recognised she was struggling and took the time and additional support she needed to deal with her complex emotions. She accepted and worked hard to understand how she was feeling and gradually found a way forward. Six months later, she had 'bounced beyond' her adversity and wanted to use her learning to help others. She has become a mental health first aider and blogger.

The difference seemed to be that the second coachee believed she had an 'internal locus of control' where she took responsibility and felt that she could choose how to respond. The first person took a more passive approach and seemed unwilling or unable to take the action required to change his circumstances. This indicates an 'external locus of control' belief, where people can be more likely to attribute their circumstances to fate or being out of their sphere of influence. This belief is much more likely to lead to anxiety or depression.

How does resilience relate to positive ageing?

For decades, most scientific studies on ageing have focused on trying to understand what goes wrong as we get older. In recent years, a growing number of researchers at the University of California in San Francisco (UCSF) and elsewhere have started to look at what it is that allows some older people to thrive.

The following examples have been adapted from an article by Adam Piore from UCSF entitled 'The mystery of the super ager'.

The UCSF studies have included different groups of 'agers'.

Those with the highest cognitive and functional performance for their age were termed 'resilient agers' and there certainly seems to be some evidence to suggest a mind-body connection. Those with a positive mental attitude and a more optimistic outlook on life even seemed to be able to counteract some of the physical symptoms of ageing.

Elissa Epel, PhD, a Professor of Psychology who co-directs the UCSF Ageing, Metabolism and Emotions Center, believes one's chronological age and biological age do not always align. More research is in progress to try and ascertain what makes some agers more resilient than others. One of the factors seems to be the ability to handle stress. Greater resilience can act as a buffer against stress and can even slow down the ageing process.

An example is given of an anonymous candidate studied as part of their research. In his late eighties, his brain scans showed significant cognitive degeneration. Yet he was still able to think and function in a much younger way. When he was interviewed, what was apparent was his positive outlook on life and his gratitude for everything he had. He was an active volunteer in the community and had close family relationships. He talked about 'not sweating the small stuff' and keeping life in perspective.

It is exciting to hear that there is evidence emerging to support the theory of mind over matter when it comes to ageing. This anonymous candidate illustrates literally the power of a positive mindset and practices like gratitude, volunteering and keeping life in perspective to increase resilience and 'rewire the brain' despite tangible signs of deterioration.

The following example also highlights the advantages of a positive outlook.

> *Case study*
> An elderly neighbour, in his eighties, who still plays golf several times a week, told me this story:
>
> "Boarding school at thirteen and National Service at eighteen were great moulders in my case and certainly gave me a positive outlook on life. This served me well, when later in my career my company suffered severe losses and I had to join their hardship fund. I had to sell my house and downsize. Several colleagues could not cope and took their own lives. It was a time to keep a stiff upper lip and positive attitude – with a supportive wife and family, we found a delightful small cottage and have lived there happily ever since."

What else does the research say?

Once again, we can turn to Japanese culture to learn more. One of the observations made in *ikigai* is that when people have a purpose in life, they pursue their passion no matter what, often overcoming many obstacles. This is resilience and grit in action.

The Japanese believe that resilience is an outlook that can be cultivated and which can protect us against negative emotions. Findings from the UCSF reinforce the theory that negative attitudes to ageing can cause people to become more stress reactive and less stress resilient, which can accelerate the ageing process. So, a vicious cycle or self-fulfilling prophecy can be the result of negative emotions.

We have already looked at the claim that positive psychology is a buffer against mental illness and the work of Barbara Fredrickson outlines the benefits of cultivating more positive emotions to minimise the impact of negativity. Now it seems as though resilience has added benefits in our later years. Highly resilient people live longer and believe their life is more meaningful.

> '92% of those with high resilience said their life had meaning in contrast to only 2% of those with low resilience who said their life had meaning.'
> – Resilience Center

I also like Liggy Webb's bite-sized book entitled *Resilience: How to cultivate inner strength and bounce ability*, in which she talks about embracing 'probortunities' by turning problems into opportunities. Sometimes it really is about how you perceive things, and if we build our resilience, we often feel stronger and more able to see things differently.

> 'Remember that sometimes not getting what you want is a wonderful stroke of luck!'
> – Dalai Lama

Resilience from good times

In Matthew Johnstone's *The Little Book of Resilience,* he talks about 'creating strength and mental fortitude by going through tough positive experiences'. Examples of this might include completing a qualification, running a marathon or even having a child. All these challenges require determination and willingness to learn from setbacks, but what a feeling of pride and achievement when we have done it. You only have to look at some of our most competitive sportsmen and women – think Mo Farah or Serena Williams – to see the buzz gained by 'pushing out of their comfort zone'.

For me, one of my greatest achievements has been raising twin daughters, which has pushed my own boundaries and developed skills and resources I never knew I had. So, when I am faced with a tough challenge now, I often look back on the early days of sleepless nights and developing new parenting skills to reassure myself that I can do it.

Beyond resilience

We have already mentioned the fact that some people can come through adversity even stronger and the concept of 'post-traumatic growth'. Only the other day, I read about a young man diagnosed with genetic early onset dementia in his twenties who said he had become a better person for knowing this as he was much more compassionate to others.

Think of a muscle fibre which is torn when overused and grows back stronger when it repairs – this is the concept of 'antifragility' coined by Nassim Nicholas Taleb in his book

Antifragile: Things That Gain from Disorder. He defines antifragility as beyond resilience or robustness.

My coaching client who lost her husband to suicide would not have wished this on her worst enemy but sees herself as stronger because of her experience and the resources she found within herself to deal with it.

One of the best role models I can think of in terms of 'post-traumatic growth' is Melanie Reid, *The Times* columnist and author who became tetraplegic after falling from her horse. Her Spinal Column, which appears weekly in Saturday's *Times Magazine*, is searingly honest about her experiences and pulls no punches. She does not shy away from the reality of her daily life and some of the inevitable negative emotions. She uses honesty, insight and humour to engage the reader. One of my favourite columns was the one where she struggled alone for *two* hours to take off her 'posh coat', almost suffocating in the attempt, after coming home early from her friend's funeral. Talk about resilience and grit – *respect*.

Reid has actively chosen to challenge her disability daily and describes her writing as a form of therapy which helped her regain her power and paid the bills. She has used her writing in a broader sense to raise awareness of living with a disability and was awarded an honorary degree from the University of Stirling 'in recognition of her contribution to journalism, to disability rights and awareness, and for being an inspirational example of human resilience and dignity'. She was also awarded an MBE in 2016 for services to journalism and to people with disabilities.

Summary

So, there is considerable evidence to suggest that being resilient is an invaluable asset in terms of positive ageing. The good news is that it can be fostered and actively honed throughout our lives. At the beginning of this chapter, we talked about resilience as being a lynchpin for many of the other characteristics defined in this book. In fact, they are all interconnected. Shoring ourselves up before we experience some of the losses and challenges of old age would seem like a wise investment, not least for the reasons below:

Key learnings

- Highly resilient people live longer.
- A resilient and positive mindset can counteract some of the physical symptoms of ageing.
- Resilience can be developed from both good and bad experiences.
- Resilience and determination combined with a passion or purpose seems likely to encourage people to redouble their efforts in the face of adversity.
- It is possible to become 'even stronger' as a result of difficult experiences. This can be described as antifragility or post-traumatic growth.

So how resilient are you?

With all these advantages to becoming more resilient, you may want to check out your own levels of resilience before targeting areas you could develop.

Complete the 'What's your resilience quota?' questionnaire below and then the activities to build your resilience.

What's your resilience quota?

Using a scale of 1-10 (1 being low, 10 being high), please rate yourself against the following statements:

1. Most of the time, my self-belief is high and I feel capable of overcoming my problems.

2. People would describe me as an optimistic person.

3. I usually bounce back fairly quickly after stressful situations.

4. I am generally flexible and can adapt to new situations.

5. I don't beat myself up when things don't work out as well as I'd hoped.

6. I can usually find something to laugh about.

7. I stay focused, calm and think clearly under pressure.

8. I am in touch with my emotions and can handle negative feelings.

9. I know when I need help and where to find it.

10. I always try and learn from difficult experiences.

11. I know what undermines my resilience and I have strategies in place to stop getting derailed.

12. I am usually able to keep things in perspective.

Adapted from Resilience Questionnaire – LBD Associates Ltd

Scoring and next steps

1. Notice your higher scores and acknowledge the areas where you feel most resilient. Feel justifiably proud of the things you do well.
2. Identify one or two of your lower scores, where you want to increase your resilience. See these as a work in progress.
3. Make a note of these and as you read each chapter, write down any tips and techniques you want to incorporate. You may find the following activities helpful:

Activities

Building your resilience muscle

1) Energisers and drainers

Get rid of self-sabotaging habits that make you vulnerable to stress. For example, make a list of five things that 'drain' your energy and five things which you find uplifting and energising. Your list of 'drainers' might include:

- One-way friends who 'suck you dry' (energy vampires)
- A dirty or cluttered work or home environment
- A debt or obligation you have left unpaid
- Clothes which don't fit but which you hang onto 'just in case'
- A phone call or email you have been putting off

Recognise the impact these are having on your state of mind and feelings of strength and resilience. Resolve to deal with them and write a date for action against each drainer.

Now identify five energisers: things which give you a boost and make you feel good. My own include:

- Yoga or meditation
- Meeting up with 'two-way' friends
- Watching a favourite film
- Listening to music
- A delicious coffee

Make a plan for how you can fit in at least one or two of these every day. Notice the impact this has on your mood.

2) Become your own life coach
Start to treat yourself as kindly as you would a friend. Ask yourself the following questions on a weekly basis and make notes of your answers:

- What have you achieved this week that you are proud of?
- How are you going to reward yourself for these achievements?
- What, if anything, do you need to forgive yourself for? What did you learn from this?

We are often much harder on ourselves than we would be on others and rarely reflect on our achievements or treat ourselves with kindness. Practise this for a month and see if you feel any different.

3) Build emotional resilience

All emotions are valid – none are good or bad; they are just giving us information. Yet, often we tell ourselves we 'shouldn't' feel a certain way – angry, sad or afraid – when very often there is a good reason for doing so.

There is evidence to suggest that 'labelling' and speaking the emotion out loud can often diffuse the power of it and enable you to move on.

So, let's imagine you are upset by the way someone has treated you. Rather than ignore the feeling, speak it out loud: "Well, no wonder I'm feeling upset! I know John probably didn't mean to offend me when he asked if I'd put weight on, but I was still hurt."

Often, you may decide not to do anything about it. However, sometimes, by validating the emotion it can enable you to keep it in perspective and move on more quickly – a useful skill for us sensitive types!

Another strategy covered on Langley Group's excellent programme on Emotional Intelligence is the Four A's: Awareness, Acceptance, Adjustment and Action:

Awareness – notice what you are feeling and try and 'label' the emotion.

Acceptance – recognise that the emotion is valid and has a message.

Adjustment – decide then if it is appropriate to express your anger, fear, disgust etc. in that moment.

Action – take the action you need to diffuse or 'park' it for the time being and decide how you will deal with it later (talk to someone, journal or a long walk).

Try this next time a strong emotion engulfs you at an inappropriate moment and see what happens.

Four

Proactivity

'Some people want it to happen, some wish it
would happen – others make it happen.'
– Michael Jordan

What is proactivity and why is it important?

Does the quote above ring true for you? Or are you one of
those people who have more of a challenge committing to
what you say you're going to do?

The Cambridge Dictionary defines proactivity as 'taking
action to make changes yourself rather than reacting to
things that happen'.

It means taking control and making things happen
rather than hiding your head in the sand and waiting for
the inevitable to befall you. Proactivity involves a degree of
autonomy and independent thinking and is also indicative
of a good sense of self-worth. Being prepared can
alleviate problems by pre-empting or minimising them.
Anticipating problems and taking appropriate action can

also leave time to deal with the unexpected things outside of your control.

Having an optimistic outlook that things will work out well and a sense of purpose with clear goals can also help people feel more proactive, so hopefully previous chapters will have left you feeling ready to initiate more action.

'I own my problems – they don't own (or define) me.'
– Anon

Proactive people tend to be more relaxed, prepared and positive as they have anticipated the 'what ifs'. They feel as though they have more control over their own future and destiny.

Things happen in life that we are not prepared for. For example, in the past, our parents' generation 'saved for a rainy day' (a proactive behaviour), whereas we are now much more prepared to borrow or live with debt and often react in the moment rather than planning for the future.

What happens if we are not proactive?

Reactive people respond as problems arise, rather than anticipating them. They are often more stressed, living from crisis to crisis and feeling 'badly done to' or backed into a corner with limited solutions to unexpected problems. We all know people who live their lives like this, and they can be chaotic to work for or live with.

Generally, reactive people blame their circumstances or other people for things they feel they have no control over.

They do not feel powerful or autonomous and may be more susceptible to low mood or depression.

Proactive people don't blame others for their problems – they take responsibility for their own behaviour and actions. They appear more confident, often calmer and more in control. Generally speaking, they can differentiate between things within their sphere of influence (e.g. things they have some control over) and take opportunities to try and influence others about important issues, which might shift their perspective. They don't waste time or energy worrying about things outside of their control (e.g. the weather, other people's reactions). As a result of working on things they can control, their sphere of influence grows. Mahatma Gandhi, the Indian leader and social activist, is often quoted as a good example of someone who worked in this way. He had no official status or position, yet his influence and impact were legendary.

So, it is not surprising that Dr Stephen Covey's eminent book *The 7 Habits of Highly Effective People* defines 'Be Proactive' as the first of seven very useful strategies for managing life. Without this, we may not have the will to practise the others.

> 'The proactive approach to a mistake is to acknowledge it instantly, correct and learn from it.'
> – Stephen R. Covey

Proactive people are much easier company both in the workplace and at home. They make good leaders and instil confidence in others.

I run a programme called 'Whose career is it anyway?' to encourage people to be more proactive about managing their own career plans. A surprising number of people in corporate life still believe that if they keep their heads down and work hard, this will automatically be noticed and lead to promotion. Well guess what? Nobody cares as much about your career as you do, and making sure people are aware of your ambitions and appropriate self-promotion are much more likely to get the desired results.

The more passive people learn this the hard way.

How does proactivity relate to positive ageing?

This same approach applies to ageing. We can just let it happen to us or we can put ourselves in the driving seat. 'Whose ageing process is it anyway?' could well be a good workshop title.

In an ideal world, by the time we reach the second half of life, we will have gained the wisdom and perspective required to act where needed. This is neatly summed up by the Serenity Prayer:

'God grant me the serenity to accept the things
I cannot change, courage to change the things I
can and wisdom to know the difference.'
– Reinhold Niebuhr

Knowing where you can make a difference and accepting what may be outside of your control is a particularly important attribute for positive agers.

Case study

My friend Helen was widowed in her late sixties and was left in a beautiful house in quite an isolated area, which was a car ride away from most places she needed to go to. When she hit her mid-seventies, she realised that her eyesight was getting worse, and she was no longer such a confident driver. She also became a little less steady on her feet. So, she decided to act and found herself a lovely new place in the heart of town, near her local church and with a ready-made community around her. She sold her car and can now walk into town for shopping, the library, coffee with friends and is a popular member of the community. She still gives a temporary home to those in need and provides occasional after-school care for neighbours' children. She also found herself a yoga teacher to improve her strength and balance and sought expert advice on her eye problems, investing in fabulous new glasses.

Not surprisingly, she has a number of friends who genuinely enjoy her company and are happy to provide occasional lifts when required. Largely independent yet not afraid to ask for help when needed, Helen manages the fine balance between independence and dependence well.

Contrast Helen's approach with a sad and frightened elderly aunt of friends of ours. She refused to accept that her small flat was going to be sold to and demolished by property developers. Leaving things to the very last minute not only narrowed her options but also impacted hugely on our friends, who had to make several trips to Israel in a short space of time to get her moved.

This highlights a major benefit of being proactive in later years. Very few of us would deliberately want to become a burden to our friends or family. Yet by avoiding taking pre-emptive steps to adapt life as needed, that is often what we may become.

> 'Research shows that *perceived control* – a measure that reflects individuals' sense of control over their lives – is closely associated with *life satisfaction* in older age.'
> – Ploubidis et al, 2011

Case study
Another example of proactive behaviour is the ninety-four-year-old man who featured recently on a TV programme about ageing. He goes to the gym

four times a week and looks much younger than his years. I had to smile, as when he was interviewed, he said: "The thing is, I took a look at myself in the mirror when I was sixty-five and didn't like what I saw, so I decided to do something about it." Bravo!

What gets in the way?

It's never too late to take action, but how many of us delay, procrastinate or put off the things we *say* we really want to do?

This book is a good example. I have talked about writing a book for years, done interviews, researched widely, even written book proposals, and still no writing was done. A box of research and ideas sat gathering dust in my office.

One Christmas, a good friend, who writes for her living, bought me a book called *How To Write Non-Fiction: Turn Your Knowledge Into Words* by Joanna Penn. She attached a message saying, 'if not now, when?'. This quote, often attributed to Ronald Reagan, brought me up short. It is something I often use when coaching clients, so the irony of 'not walking my talk' was not lost on me. Thank you, Erika, for jolting me out of my inertia and for your invaluable help with this book.

Being proactive may also sometimes mean coming out of our comfort zone and challenging outdated beliefs, which may no longer serve us well.

In one of my old favourite books *Feel the Fear and Do It Anyway*, Susan Jeffers talks about the need to reframe some of our 'old assumptions' such as 'don't ask for help' or 'don't take risks' etc.

This is especially true in later years. How often does pride, stubbornness or an old belief that you need to do everything yourself stop older people asking for or accepting the help they clearly need? During the 2020 Covid-19 pandemic, I met several people who felt uncomfortable at suddenly being defined as 'elderly and vulnerable'. Yet many were humbled and grateful for the support that was available to them. What they may not have realised is that the helpers often get just as much out of this sense of giving (more on this in chapter eight on connectivity).

This transition from helper to being helped often seems difficult for older people to accept. It may be made easier by anticipating some of the adjustments needed in later life, and taking a more proactive approach could help people feel more in control of their own destiny.

What the research says

So, what is it that enables some people to feel more motivated to be proactive and take action, and what causes other people to procrastinate or avoid taking action until events force them to?

One theory of human motivation we learned about on our DPP programme was self-determination theory (SDT) developed by psychologists Edward Deci and Richard Ryan.

Deci and Ryan claim that humans are proactive by nature and are capable of mastering their own motivations and behaviours. They highlight three core needs that facilitate this kind of mindset:

Autonomy – to feel like we have control over what we do.

Competence – to feel like we can be effective when taking action.

Relatedness – to have meaningful relationships and interactions with others.

Once these three needs are satisfied, they promote intrinsic motivation which also builds resilience and enables people to operate at their best.

Intrinsic motivation is much more likely to lead to proactive behaviour as people understand the benefits to themselves and feel better for taking action. Those who rely on extrinsic motivations appear more likely to rely on rewards (or threats) from others to act. Fear of change and the unknown is also likely to play a part here (see chapter five on adaptability).

Proactive approach to health and well-being

Nowhere is proactivity more relevant than with our own health and well-being. There is an increasing need for people to take more responsibility for managing their own health to take the strain off the overstretched National Health Service (NHS).

I, for one, welcome this approach and feel very fortunate to have an enlightened GP with whom I work in partnership. I am proactive enough to educate myself about specific health concerns and options for managing these so that we can have a more informed discussion when I visit. I am also not afraid to ask for what I need, or to ask for alternatives if medication is discussed. I recognise this requires confidence and willingness to take responsibility. I have been pleasantly surprised at how many tests are available on the NHS if you ask and know why you want them. I am also curious and open-minded about complementary treatments and therapies, which can often add value to traditional approaches. Craniosacral therapy (see chapter one on sense of purpose) is a good example of this, and I have added monthly treatments into my health maintenance routine.

Whether this approach will pay off in the long term is not guaranteed, but it certainly makes me feel more in control and less fearful about the future. Having a proactive approach can help people feel more positive, even if that means on occasions accepting the facts and working with a diagnosis rather than fighting against it or living in denial. It is often the agony of not knowing or uncertainty which can paralyse us. Google can be a mixed blessing in these instances, often fuelling our imagination to expect the worst. Not surprisingly, health anxiety is on the increase.

There is a growing trend towards each of us having a more proactive (and hopefully preventive) personalised healthcare plan, and there are a few patient-friendly books which I have found very informative in widening my knowledge in this area. These are listed at the end of the book.

Case study

Norman is now in his mid-seventies. He was widowed two years ago after spending many years caring devotedly for his wife who succumbed to dementia. When he retired, they moved to the coast where the sea air and beach walks provided a healthier environment. He struggled with the 24/7 demands, which took their toll on his energy. He gave up drinking, recognising this was not helping his own health and mood. To his great credit his wife died in their own home. Norman rang to tell us as he was walking along the beach recalling happy memories he and his wife had shared. He then became very proactive: had a knee replacement, worked hard to lose weight, rejoined his golf club and took up shooting. He has kept his mischievous sense of humour, counts his blessings and does good turns for his neighbours. He is one of my favourite role models for positive ageing, and I always enjoy his company.

One word of warning about taking too much control of your health – be aware of your own personality here and whether knowing too much will make you worry more about things you may not be able to control. For example, gene testing is in the early stages of development and soon it may be possible to find out how we could die. Some of us (optimists) may think that by being better informed we can make lifestyle adjustments to minimise the risks (e.g. Angelina Jolie having radical surgery to try and reduce chances of breast cancer). However, if you have an anxious personality, you may prefer not to know. Being preoccupied with health could lead to unhealthy consequences.

Again, I'd like to share a personal story. When I was pregnant with non-identical twins many years ago, I was offered an amniocentesis test. I agonised about having this, knowing it brought a slight risk of miscarriage and also wondering how I would feel if one baby was adversely affected. The question which made up my mind was this: if you don't have this test, will you spend the rest of your pregnancy worrying about it?

The answer was yes and so I went ahead, feeling forewarned was forearmed, and was extremely fortunate to find out I was carrying healthy twin girls. I have talked to several people since who would not have wanted to know or taken that chance. As I said, knowing yourself is really important.

Summary

Being proactive is a lifestyle choice with many benefits, among them being more prepared and less fearful about the future. It is also a trait worth developing if you want to feel more positive about ageing – there are usually choices and potential solutions to most of the challenges in later life, once we are more informed.

Even things you don't want to think about can feel less scary when out in the open. A friend sat down with her two teenage children and asked them to consider what kind of funeral they would have. She then shared her wishes, so they were all prepared.

Becoming more proactive is possible with practice. See below for activity suggestions.

Key learnings
- Proactive people feel more in control.
- Being proactive can help to reduce stress levels.
- Taking a proactive approach to health issues can mean earlier diagnosis and treatment plans.

Activities

How to become more proactive
Here are three activities which might help you do this:

1) Clearing the decks
What jobs have you been avoiding?
How might that be affecting your energy?
How would you feel if you tackled these?
Make a list of five tasks that have been on the bottom of your to-do list and then a date by which you will have actioned them. My own list looks like this:

What I've been putting off doing	When I will action this?
• Sort out old photos	• Bank Holiday weekend
• Clear inbox of old emails	• By end of this week
• Ring a friend I've lost touch with	• Tomorrow
• Book a Pilates lesson	• Tomorrow
• Try a new recipe	• This weekend

2) The worry list

I find this a good way of getting worries 'out of my head' and then deciding which ones are within or outside of my control.

Step one: take a large sheet of paper and brainstorm every little thing you are worried about – don't censor anything. It can include anything, big or small, from getting older to wondering if your mum is taking her medication to what on earth you are going to buy someone for a special birthday. Just write until you can think of no more.

Step two: now take three different colour pens and mark each one against these criteria.

- Is it in my control? (mark with a C)
- Is it out of my direct control but I may be able to influence it? (mark with an I)

- Is it something I'm concerned about but out of my control? (mark with an X)

Step three:

a. First take all your items marked with a 'C' against them and ask yourself what *action* you can take to minimise this worry, e.g. for your friend's birthday you can do some online research, ask people who know her well for ideas etc.

b. Then take your items marked with an 'I' against them and consider how you might be able to influence other people to take *action* on this, e.g. you could enlist the support of a neighbour/carer to call in regularly to be with your mother while she takes her medication.

c. Finally, take a look at your items marked with an X and consider if there is *anything* you can do which would make your worry less, e.g. getting older – whilst we can't turn back the clock, we can take some actions which may help make this a less worrying experience.

See below for an example of how you might want to summarise these and prioritise those within your control.

Sample worry list

Worry	In My Control "C"	Influence "I"	Out of My Control "X"	Action
Friend's poor health		I		Do some research; keep in regular touch and phone more often
Work project	C			Plan ahead, get organised, set deadlines and delegate some jobs
Family member's significant birthday celebration		I		Involve others, investigate options and find out what they want
Climate Change			X	Educate myself, make small changes to my lifestyle
Too much screen time	C			Delete some Apps. Be more disciplined with e-mails and plan in regular digital "detox" time

3) Scenario planning

Consider a forthcoming change or possibility which is weighing on your mind. This may be a potential job change, house move, impending operation, losing someone close to you etc. The motto here is 'be prepared'.

Take some time out and a large sheet of paper to consider three things:

Best case scenario – how would you like things to look in an ideal world? Write down or draw what this would look and feel like.

Worst case scenario – face your fears and write or draw the worst possible outcome you can imagine. Then ask yourself the following question: if this did happen, could I handle it? More often than not, the fear of something is worse than the reality, and if you force yourself to consider how you would cope, some of the anxiety may subside.

Most likely scenario – be honest and realistic with yourself to consider that your best hopes and worst fears might not be realised, and the most likely outcome may lie somewhere in-between. Again, write down or draw what this looks and feels like for you.

This is a powerful activity and one which can help you keep things in perspective and feel more prepared.

Five

Adaptability

'It is not the strongest of the species that survives, nor the most intelligent. It is the one that is most adaptable to change.'
– Charles Darwin

What is adaptability and why is it important?

Adaptability is defined as 'the quality of being able to adjust to new conditions'. It is the ability to accept change and to let go of the past, knowing what you can control and being able to manage the conflicting emotions which often accompany a shift in circumstances.

One of my elderly friends, admittedly with hindsight, described being widowed: "I just accepted that was a chapter of my life that was finished, and it was time to move on." Needless to say, she was also proactive and able to keep life in perspective.

Let me contrast that with another elderly friend of ours who is still 'stuck in the past', and twelve years after losing his wife to cancer still has her clothes hanging in the wardrobe. It is very sad to see him unwilling to get the help he needs to move on and, inevitably, it has affected his health. Whilst he seems old at seventy, my other friend is a young eighty-seven.

The reason adaptability is so important at any age is that it takes deliberate effort, as many human beings are hardwired to resist change. Some of the science behind this maintains that by the time we get to a certain age, we have formed a mental model of how we see the world and how we think it should be, which fits with our core beliefs ('The Science Behind Why We Fail to Adapt' – Greg Satell). It is difficult for us to shift from this, especially if we do not have a well-formed view of what the change might bring. Change can be difficult, and it often seems much easier to stay in our comfort zone.

Change can also bring loss and unless we can compensate for this with at least some idea of the benefits a change might bring then it can be difficult to take the leap of faith required to embrace new circumstances. Even bereavement can eventually offer the freedom to live a different life.

Julia Samuels, the eminent British psychotherapist, has written an excellent book on loss and grief called *This Too Shall Pass*. One thing we know is that life consists of continuous change, and I believe everyone would benefit from mastering the life skill of managing change more effectively.

The Change Curve

I remember well that the first time I learned about the Change Curve (see below) and the emotional roller coaster this can bring, I felt relieved. I wasn't going mad – there was a reason for those difficult feelings.

I have run many training workshops on this topic and the 'dip in the curve' is always a phase people can relate to. One of the things which determines how long you stay in the dip is how proactive you are prepared to be and how much support you have to get through it.

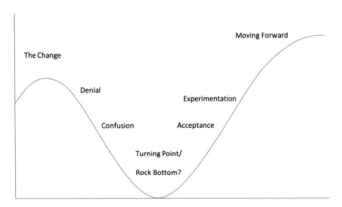

CHANGE CURVE MODEL

Adapted from the Kubler-Ross model on the Five Stages of Grief

Adaptability is a quality that can really help us to process and navigate change – whether we have chosen the change or not. Change is a given. The only thing we are in control of is the way we choose to respond to it. Sometimes it is the unexpected things which can make this harder.

For example, it's easy to imagine that you will have a new lease of life when your children leave home. Time to yourself, freedom to travel and less chaos to clear up are all imagined as huge advantages.

What can be unexpected is that feeling of loss – the term 'empty nest syndrome' was coined with good reason. Whilst we may have complained about having too much to do or feeling as though we were at everyone's beck and call, suddenly we have almost too much time on our hands and the house can feel quiet and empty.

It takes a while to adjust and adapt our life accordingly and, as the Change Curve illustrates, this process can bring with it a whole host of emotions. Just as we finally feel we have got our own lives on track again, back come the kids, on holiday from university or moving back home temporarily to save up for travels or a house purchase. So, we have to adjust again, this time to living with young adults, negotiating new 'house rules' if we are all to stay sane.

It's often the same for people who are made redundant. For some this comes as a shock, for others a welcome relief. However, it still brings with it a wave of mixed emotions: anger, sadness, fear and also maybe a tinge of excitement about 'what next?'. We need to adapt again and carve out a new identity outside of work or adjust to a new way of working (e.g. being a carer, going part-time, setting up a business etc.).

Sometimes the emotions of fear and excitement can evoke similar responses in the body. Think of the 'butterflies in the tummy' feeling before an important event or meeting. I try to remember this if I feel nervous about something.

I must admit, I'm not always that good at adapting to change myself. Writing this chapter encouraged me to look back on the many changes I have experienced in life and reflect on how I handled them. One that sticks in my mind is moving to Canada to live for two years. It was exciting, fun and a welcome change which brought real quality family time and plenty of travelling. What I was totally unprepared for was moving back to the UK, and it took me a long time to settle. As a result of my experiences, I had a different perspective on life and yet I was trying to fit back into the same lifestyle and job. It was the catalyst I needed to leave corporate life and set up my own business, which would have seemed too risky before Canada.

> 'We can only embrace the future if we are willing to make the effort to break free of the past.'
> – Greg Satell

This also requires the ability and willingness to 'unlearn and relearn' and be more open-minded about new ways of being and working.

As futurist and philosopher Alvin Toffler once wrote: 'the illiterate of the 21st century will not be those who cannot read and write, but those who cannot learn, unlearn, and relearn'.

Nowhere is this truer than in the world of work. According to Catherine DeVrye, the seven most expensive words in business are: 'we have always done it that way'.

Taking a different direction

'We can't control everything that happens, but we
can change our experience of those things.'
– Headspace

Do you ever look back at a time when things didn't work
out as you had wanted and think, *thank goodness*? This
might include not getting a job you had set your heart
on, or having a long-planned trip cancelled, or things not
working out in a relationship. Whilst you might have been
disappointed at the time, often something better may have
come along.

Adaptability and keeping an open mind can really
help here. Maybe things weren't meant to be, and life has a
different plan for you. Sometimes this means giving up the
need to feel in control of *everything* and just going with the
flow, trusting that things will work out.

A friend passed on this lovely rhyme from her mum:

'Don't whittle and worry, don't dither and doubt – just count up
the times things have worked themselves out.'
– Source unknown

When my daughter went off on her own to Australia for a gap
year, her goals were to live and work in a different country,
to travel and to learn. She arrived during the bush fires. She
moved cities to find work. Soon she found work where she

was valued and which allowed her to save. Shortly afterwards, the world was hit by the coronavirus crisis and many people were 'let go' from their jobs, including her. Lockdown was challenging – her flatmate moved on, and with dwindling savings, she was forced to reconsider her options. Come back to the UK or consider farm work in a different area, which might enable her to extend her visa and still fulfil her travel plans. The prospects back in the UK were bleak, and although farm work was well out of her comfort zone, she gave it a go. It was not for her. So, she reconsidered, took bar work and travelled on a shoestring, returning to the UK a couple of months early. She was forced to adapt and change her plans several times, and I was very proud of her. As she said, she went for an adventure – it just may not have been quite the adventure she had in mind. Whilst you may well wonder what this example has to do with positive ageing, imagine what it was like to be ten thousand miles away and on the receiving end of hearing about all these changes with resulting ups and downs. I felt as though I went through the Change Curve many times myself while trying to keep upbeat for my daughter.

What happens if we don't have adaptability?

Some elderly people can't accept that they need to action some lifestyle changes to make the next phase easier for themselves and others. They focus on what they have lost or can't do, rather than making the most of what they still have.

One of the things I notice is how hard on themselves some older people can be, constantly pointing out their shortcomings or harping back to the past when they used to have better mobility, memories or more hair. Understandably, these people don't seem to enjoy life as much, and can be inclined to depression.

If we think back to that Change Curve, it can be very tempting to stay in the denial phase, not facing up to the fact that things need to change. We can be blind to the warning signs of needing to adapt, even when others can see this quite clearly. For example, defiant smokers who imagine they are immune to the dangers, or people who are seriously overweight who are seemingly oblivious to the health risks. No one can pretend that change is easy or that adapting a lifestyle you've enjoyed for many years comes naturally. But what happens if we don't adapt?

Life can become increasingly uncomfortable, causing stress and poor health. For example, I am struck by the number of people who refuse to wear the glasses they clearly need or get the hearing test that might save a great deal of shouting and improve relationships with their nearest and dearest. Don't they realise that wrinkles that might result from straining to see or missing out on conversations can be much more ageing than the alternatives?

Yes, denial is a tempting place to reside, and the future can look bleak for many. On a more positive note, whether it was denial or not, my friend's father (now in his nineties) just imagined he was going blonder when he first started to go grey. He still drives and sees himself as a 'babe magnet'!

Case study

A friend's grandmother was 105 when she died. A tough, independent old lady, she lived on her own in the Canadian mountains, brewing her own beer. The only concession my friend can remember her making to getting older is that the family finally got her to stop going onto the roof to mend the snow damage.

Case study

An elderly neighbour told me there was nothing good about getting old. His wife, on the other hand, who had dementia, was thankful for what she had and always said there were people much worse off. Easy to dismiss this as an optimist married to a pessimist, but it may also say as much about the mental health of carers. She also outlived him despite her condition.

There are some sad stories about people who just 'give up' when they are faced with a life change that they find unacceptable. For example, going into a care home, whilst it may not be a popular choice, can either bring a new lease of life or result in a marked deterioration in health and well-being.

Case study

A friend was forced to make the difficult decision to put her dear dad into care. He did not go willingly and complained every time she went to visit. However, secretly, he began to enjoy himself, surrounded by ladies and getting plenty of attention. It wasn't long before he met a special lady friend who made his last years very happy. A lovely example of life taking a different turn of events even when it wasn't a popular choice.

If people fail to make the adjustment to being retired, it can result in poor health:

> 'Too many of us define ourselves by our work. When that goes, many are left bereft. People can feel lost, which puts the body and mind under considerable strain. Rates of death and ill-health peak after retirement.'
> – Max Pemberton

> 'Retirement was difficult – I loved my work and the interchange with colleagues. Suddenly, it was all over. One becomes the unseen, the invisible, the old bloke down the street.'
> – Mr Garry

What better time to create a new life plan and find a different sense of purpose? (see chapter one). We will come back to Mr Garry in a later chapter.

What does the research say?

So, given all the advantages of being more adaptable, how can we develop more of this quality?

I'd like to consider this with a particular emphasis on whether we can develop a more flexible mindset and become more open to change.

Carol Dweck, an American psychologist, has developed an interesting theory about fixed and growth mindsets, which, while not without its critics, has become popular in mainstream education.

Simply put, this theory is that those with a fixed mindset believe their levels of intelligence or talents are inherently 'fixed' and will not change. They accept the status quo and might say things like: 'I don't have a musical bone in my body so I will never be able to sing'.

Those people with a growth mindset believe in continuous learning and improvement and that their intrinsic levels of ability can be developed through hard work. They constantly strive for better and might say things like: 'I've never had singing lessons but with practice I think I would be good at it'.

From her research, Dweck discovered a difference between how children responded to difficult work which was just beyond their current capability.

Those with a fixed mindset tended to give up more easily, thinking it was just too hard for them. Those with a growth mindset tended to be excited by the challenge and strived to work things out, firing a different kind of brain activity.

This concept is described in more detail in Carol Dweck's book *Mindset: The New Psychology of Success.*

How does this apply to positive ageing?

I believe this theory can equally be applied to our super agers. Whilst some people accept the challenges that getting older might bring as an inevitable part of the ageing process and narrow their lives accordingly, those with a 'growth mindset' fully believe that they can have a positive influence and make things better. It is as if they tell themselves different stories and can imagine new possibilities. With practice, it is perfectly possible to challenge our automatic thinking patterns, especially if these are negative, and to disrupt them with a more open-minded approach.

For example, cognitive behavioural therapy (CBT) is a short-term goal-oriented psychotherapy treatment with a hands-on practical approach to problem-solving. Its goal is to change patterns of thinking or behaviour that are behind people's difficulties and change the way they feel. It has become very popular for treating mild depression and mood disorders, and I know many people who have benefitted from a short course in CBT. Quite simply, if you learn to shift your thinking patterns, it can alter your behaviour and so make a difference to how you feel. There is an argument that this is a life skill we should all learn, and it is a good example of how the brain can be rewired.

Challenging perceptions

'Late life becomes an opportunity for new
imaginings, looking forward and backward to the
lives we have lived and still might live.'
– Professor Molly Andrews

A couple of years ago, I visited a fascinating exhibition at the Barbican called Unclaimed Conversations. This was an interactive installation created by The Liminal Space and supported by the Wellcome Trust and Centre for Ageing Better, which presented some up-to-date statistics on age.

'Nearly 1 in 3 people currently in the UK will
live to see their 100th birthday.'
– Office for National Statistics, 2016

This was followed by a workshop facilitated by Professor Molly Andrews from the University of East London and Dr. Daniel Davis, Consultant Geriatrician at University College London Hospital, to encourage us to challenge some of our perceptions around ageing and examine the possibilities of exploring new futures based on this research.

The following two questions caused me to think quite profoundly:

- If you knew you were going to live to a hundred, how would that change your approach to life?

- If you could learn or try one new thing, what would it be and why?

The second of these questions touches on the 'growth mindset' and made me feel uncomfortable about some of my own 'fixed ideas', in particular to do with technology. Learning new things keeps us young at heart. As the world of work changes and working from home becomes ever more popular, I have adapted to new ways of working via Zoom, Teams and Facetime calls. This has brought many benefits, not least the time saved from travelling.

I would highly recommend the Unclaimed Conversation Cards from this workshop to get started on important yet often difficult conversations about ageing with yourself, your family or those you might work with.

My favourite piece of research on the effect of shifting mindset on ageing was conducted by Ellen Langer, a Harvard psychologist, many years ago. In some ways it was an unorthodox experiment, not regulated as it would need to be now. But it was 1979 and the results were so astounding that they are still talked about today. Langer also wrote a book called *Counterclockwise*, about how we can reverse the signs of ageing by altering our mindset.

Briefly, what Langer did was take a group of men in their seventies to a monastery where everything was staged to be as it would have been twenty years earlier.

They were all tested for signs of ageing before the experiment – some were stooped, others walking with canes;

some had become dependent on others doing things for them, either family or staff in a care home.

They were told to live and behave as if it were 1959. All news, TV programmes, books and magazines were from that era, as was the decor of the monastery. For a week they lived in this time warp. All conversations were about topics from that era but in the present tense. There were no mirrors to remind them of their real age and the only photos were of their twenty years younger selves. No allowances were made for any infirmities, and they were expected to be independent.

A control group lived in a similar environment, but they were only asked to reminisce about living in 1959, not act as if they were actually there.

A week later, both groups showed improvements in 'physical strength, manual dexterity, gait, posture, perception, memory, cognition, taste sensitivity, hearing and vision' Langer wrote in *Counterclockwise*.

According to Langer's account, the improvements were much more marked in the group told to live as if it were 1959 – 63% of them had improved scores in intelligence tests at the end of the experiment compared to 44% in the control group.

Despite the controversy surrounding the experiment, it remains a powerful example of 'mind over matter'. In other words, if you think you're old then your body might respond accordingly. It also seems likely that you can reverse some of the signs of ageing by thinking yourself young. An early example of 'ageing rewired'.

A more recent piece of evidence in *The Times* endorses the view that you are as old as you feel. Scientists have discovered that whether we feel older or younger than our chronological age crucially influences our biological age, that is how old our bodies are using some of the typical biomarkers of ageing such as walking speed, balance, grip strength, BMI, muscle mass and waist circumference. People who feel younger than their chronological age tend to be healthier and more psychologically resilient. This is certainly borne out by the majority of people interviewed or featured in this book, most of whom don't see themselves as old or 'act their age'. 'The latest research would indicate that thinking oneself young promotes healthier behaviours, such as exercising and socialising more, being open to new experiences and keeping optimistic about the future' (John Naish).

All of this absolutely resonates with some of the other chapters in this book on optimism, curiosity and connectivity. The good news is that we can all develop more of these essential characteristics.

Summary

There is evidence to support the theory that having an adaptable mindset and approach to life is beneficial to ageing more positively.

The more prepared we are to deal with whatever life may throw at us, the less likely we are to succumb to feeling like victims of circumstance.

Key learnings

- Change is a process which many humans are hardwired to resist, so it can be difficult to make a deliberate choice to respond differently.
- Understanding the Change Curve and learning techniques to manage the emotional roller coaster of change can help people adapt more easily.
- Developing a 'growth mindset' is likely to be a benefit to ageing more positively.
- The mind-body connection is powerful and can influence the ageing process positively or negatively.

How can we develop a more adaptable approach?

Activities

So how can we develop more of this quality which is so critical to making the most of later life? Here are three activities which may help:

1) Remember that sometimes not getting what you want is a wonderful stroke of luck.

Think about when this has happened to you and how things turned out better than expected. How did you have to adapt in response to this? What was the 'silver lining'? What did you learn about yourself? Write down your answers and see how you feel now about that chapter in your life.

2) What's in your tool kit?

Talk to a friend about a change that might be coming up in your life and which you're not looking forward to. This might include a health challenge, kids leaving home, divorce, losing your job etc.

Now think of a change you've already navigated in your past such as moving house, starting a new job, taking on additional caring responsibilities etc. How did you get through this?

Take time to tell your story and ask your friend to make notes against the following headings about what they noticed that helped you do this:

Attributes – skills, qualities and characteristics which served you well.

Resources – who or where you turned to for support.

Tactics – approaches or strategies you used to help you through this.

Get your friend to feed back what they heard and then make your own list of personal resources which will serve you well going forward. Refer to these when you are finding it hard to accept or adjust to something.

3) Applying a 'growth mindset'

Step one: which areas in your life might you have a 'fixed mindset' about?

Example: I'm not sporty, musical, good at maths etc.

Step two: what would happen if you applied a 'growth mindset' here?

Example: well, I've never thought of myself as particularly sporty, but I'd like to try and learn golf so that I could have a game with my husband.

Step three: what is the first step you need to take to make this happen?

Example: download a tutorial for beginners to golf.

Six

Perspective

'There are always flowers for those who want to see them.'
– Probably Henri Matisse

What is perspective and why is it important?

'A particular way of thinking about something, especially
one that is influenced by beliefs and experiences.'
– collinsdictionary.com

People who have a healthy sense of perspective don't sweat
the small stuff. They look at life as a whole and are able to be
balanced. They don't dwell on things – they either deal with
something or let it go.

'I celebrate each day. I remember the past but never live
in it or yearn for it. I live in the present, embrace the here
and now and think not of the future because that which
one may worry about may never happen.'
– Mr Garry

'Don't think too much about the future and don't dwell about what it may hold. That will come anyway so let it look after itself.'
– A friend's mother, age ninety

'Yesterday's the past, tomorrow's the future, but today is a gift. That's why it's called the present.'
– Bil Keane

I must confess I am not naturally one of those people who are easily able to keep things in perspective. Emotions play a big role for me, which can be a strength in my work as a coach but not always helpful in other ways. For example, my emotions can be heightened in response to something which others perceive as quite trivial, and I can overreact and get things out of perspective. Fortunately, I am married to a down-to-earth Yorkshireman with a healthy sense of perspective. He is usually able to stop me 'catastrophising' and imagining the worst.

During a major refurbishment at home, which I was already finding quite disruptive, we hit an unexpected problem. There was a leak in the kitchen (not planned for renovation) which meant digging up the tiles and major plumbing work. The carpets in the hall were soaked. I was distraught – it felt like a significant setback, and I worried we would never be finished in time for Christmas. My recently bereaved friend came round. Whilst she sympathised, she rightly observed that 'nobody's died – all of this can be replaced' which shifted my outlook and perspective. Another of her favourite phrases is 'we are where we are' which immediately helps me look at what can be done rather than waste time and energy on regrets.

I do find that talking to others who see things differently is a great way of keeping things in perspective. I have also found understanding my personality preferences better via the Myers-Briggs Type Indicator (MBTI) very helpful and wish I had known about this years ago! See References and Resources for more details. There are also more tips about gaining perspective at the end of this chapter.

> 'When we shift our perspective our experience
> of difficult issues is transformed.'
> – Headspace

Perspective is an important attribute to have at any age, especially with all the scaremongering which can be caused by the media. Much has been written about the increase in mental health issues as social media has become a major influencer of young people. This is often written about as having negative effects on mental health, but a recent programme called *The Truth about Mental Health* put another perspective on this. Tanya Byron (psychologist and child therapist) and Alex Scott (TV presenter and ex-professional footballer) had teamed up to explore the latest science on how to improve one's mental health. They found that those people who 'passively scrolled' on social media were more likely to feel worse after doing so. However, those who were proactive and posted things, making it work for them, often got a positive boost from this.

This helped reframe my own perspective to be a little more balanced about social media.

As we saw in the previous chapter, cognitive behavioural therapy (CBT) is becoming increasingly popular at helping people challenge their negative thoughts and can give people the skills they need to keep things in perspective. The theory behind this is that if we can change our thoughts, this shifts our behaviour, and we feel differently about things. It is a process for helping people cope with anxiety, and it works.

What happens if we don't have perspective?

When people are unable to keep things in perspective, they can let one thing dominate their lives to the exclusion of all others. For example, losing a job can be taken in different ways. For some, it will be a relief or a welcome 'kick in the backside' to branch out and try something new. For others, it might feel like the end of the world. If they have been workaholics or gained most of their identity through their work, they might feel as though they have very little left. I saw this first-hand when I worked for a large retail organisation in the 1980s. At this time, it was a very paternalistic company and people tended to think they had 'jobs for life'. So, the first restructures and redundancies came as a shock. Whilst generous leaving packages, including outplacement services, were offered, many reacted as though they had been bereaved.

As counselling services manager for the outplacement services, I learnt many lessons from this. Many people had made the company the centre of their lives and had become over-reliant on them for money, status and a sense of belonging. Many, including myself, had met their partners within the business. Quite literally, the company had been their world, and my counselling team had to work hard to shift their mindset and perspective towards creating a new future.

This experience was life-changing for me. My own life perspective shifted significantly and, following many deep and meaningful discussions with my husband, we reconsidered our decision to try for a family. A couple of years later, I gave birth to twin daughters, having never thought of myself as maternal in any way. Understandably, this added a whole new dimension to our lives, and I will be forever grateful for this shift in mindset.

One of the best books I know on the topic of life balance is Susan Jeffers' classic *Feel the Fear and Do It Anyway*, which I first read nearly thirty years ago and which I'm delighted to see has been reprinted. In particular, chapter eight entitled 'How whole is your whole life?' is as relevant today as it has ever been, and I often share this with coaching clients. Jeffers points out what seems obvious in a very user-friendly way. If we only have one 'box' in our life, be that relationship, work or children, it is likely to be a really big loss if we lose that element of our life. On the other hand, if we make an effort to keep all our 'boxes' topped up, we have many other resources to shore us up in difficult times.

How does this apply to positive ageing?

There is a steady stream of depressing health warnings and statistics in the media, which can cause alarm for elderly people. For example, many people understandably have a fear of developing dementia. Both my mother and grandmother succumbed to Alzheimer's in their seventies, which makes me especially vigilant. Sometimes just a different way of expressing things can help us see things differently.

For example, I keep reading about the fact that there are currently 850,000 people with dementia in the UK and, according to the Alzheimer's Society, this is set to rise to over 1.6 million by 2040. However, this statistic made me look at things differently:

'Less than 20% of over 85s suffer from dementia.'
– Royal Society for Public Health, 2018

So, whilst I appreciate that dementia is a worldwide problem affecting over fifty million people, the fact that there is a one in five chance of getting this by the time I'm eighty-five helps me keep it in perspective. Mindful of my genetics, I'm also a firm believer in taking responsibility for making the lifestyle changes I can to minimise the risks. This includes eating healthily, exercising regularly and keeping my brain active.

I do find that many super agers are better able to keep things in perspective, not least because they have more years to look back on and remember how they came through hard times before. A good example of this is their attitude to political uncertainty and lack of direction for the future. They are able to recall post-war years and even harder times, which is helpful. This was especially true during the 2020 pandemic, and I noticed several examples of older members of a family being able to reassure younger ones who had never lived through anything like that before.

I also have two close friends who seem able to cope with major life events calmly and philosophically. One has kidney disease and is currently researching her options for dialysis. In the last ten years, she has lost a brother and sister to the disease. The other friend is waiting for two new hip replacements, having had them both done initially in her forties. She also had breast cancer five years ago. They just seem to cope with things and get on with life. In discussion with them both, I asked for their tips on keeping life in perspective. One lost her dad at thirteen; the other lost her mum at a similar age. They told me that when you have lost a parent so young, nothing else will ever seem so bad. Once again, I felt humbled.

> 'Super agers take a relaxed philosophical approach
> to life – happy at others' good fortune but satisfied
> and content with their lot in life.'
> – Max Pemberton

Another encouraging statistic shows that anxiety appears to decrease with age. For example, 48% of seventy- to seventy-four-year-olds rated anxiety levels low compared to 38% of fifty- to fifty-four-year-olds (Centre for Ageing Better).

What does the research say?

Dominique Afacan and Helen Cathcart undertook some research to challenge their own negative perceptions of ageing. They interviewed fifty 'old' people around the world, which shattered their stereotyping of ageing forever. Their findings are published in their book entitled *Bolder: Life lessons from people older and wiser than you*. I particularly liked this quote from Michael Eavis, the founder of Glastonbury Festival, who was aged eighty at the time: 'the best age of my life so far is now. I have the satisfaction of knowing I've made the most of my life. I will die happy, but not yet!'.

Both Jane Fonda, role model extraordinaire for positive ageing, and Guy Robertson, from Positive Ageing Associates, talk about the importance of doing a 'life review' as we get older.

Jane Fonda has made a Ted Talk entitled 'Life's Third Act' which is well worth a watch and only eleven minutes long. In her inimitable and humorous way, she shares some interesting research about how we can rewire the neural pathways in our brains to become more positive if we change our relationship with the past. Still curious to keep learning at eighty-two, she talks about the 'longevity revolution' and presents persuasive arguments for undertaking this work in later life. In particular, she argues for older women redefining themselves and reclaiming their power to become better role models for young women.

Guy Robertson, in his useful and practical guide entitled *How to Age Positively*, gives detailed steps on how we can conduct our own 'life review'. He cites many benefits to this, including the fact that it really helps put life in perspective. Interestingly, those who have done more reflection on their past – including lessons learned, strengths and resources remembered from challenging times, as well as forgiveness – also seem to be clearer and more motivated to create a positive plan for the future.

Whilst there are details of how to conduct a 'life review' on your own in Robertson's guide, my own experience tells me that this can be a daunting task for many, which may be best undertaken with the help of a coach, counsellor or therapist. At the very least, try and work with a friend who has patience, time and active listening skills.

'I have great respect for the past. If you don't know where you've come from, you don't know where you're going.'
– Maya Angelou

Case study
My friend John has put this into action and chose to go to therapy sessions with his eldest daughter. This has helped him let go of many things he was holding onto, and he describes it as 'righting the wrongs from the past'. As a result, his relationship with his daughter has significantly improved and he seems to have more positive energy. It has also opened up new possibilities for doing things with his extended family that he had thought might be unattainable.

Journaling is another powerful way of making sense of life. I used to write a daily journal about life's ups and downs. A wise mentor asked me if I ever reviewed my journal writing. At the time, I didn't – it had seemed like a 'brain dump' for all the powerful emotions I was feeling around the time of my parents' deaths. So, I started to take time out to review my outpourings and realised there were patterns of behaviour and also signs of progress to note. This helped me start to make sense of the past and, in effect, acted as a kind of self-therapy.

Another powerful antidote to getting things out of perspective is to challenge our negative automatic thoughts (NATs) – a term used in cognitive behavioural therapy. One of the best books I know on this subject is *Change Your Life with CBT* by Corinne Sweet.

Whilst I am not trained in CBT, I have used some of the techniques myself and with coaching clients to good effect. For example, here is a list of 'thinking traps' often referred to by therapists and sometimes called 'limiting beliefs'. Fill in the questionnaire and highlight your most common ones.

Top ten thinking traps

Consider the following common 'thinking traps' and identify at least one which undermines your confidence.

1	**Mind reading**	Imagining that you know what the other person is thinking and fearing the worst.
2	**Overthinking / overanalysing**	Going over and over things in your mind using up unnecessary energy and worrying.
3	**Catastrophising / 'awfulising'**	Making mountains out of molehills and being overly dramatic.
4	**Mental filtering**	Ignoring the positive and wearing 'gloomy spectacles', having a 'half empty' approach.
5	**Black and white / extreme thinking**	All or nothing, always or never etc.
6	**Making assumptions**	Prioritising opinions over facts, not looking at evidence.
7	**'Shoulds', 'oughts' and 'musts'**	Putting others needs before your own. Whose voice is this?
8	**Blame game**	Putting yourself or others down and making excuses.
9	**Compare and despair**	Seeing only the positives in others and not yourself.
10	**Memories**	Negative experiences in the past haunting you, fearing things may go wrong again.

Adapted from Thinking Traps questionnaire LBD Associates Ltd

My own thinking traps include catastrophising and compare and despair (boy, do I love that one!) and CBT has really helped me become more aware of when I'm falling into that train of thought and to challenge myself.

I learnt three great responses to challenge these negative automatic thoughts when I went on a positive psychology masterclass with Miriam Akhtar and Bridget Glenville-Cleave. These serve me well when I catch myself going down a negative thinking route:

1. That can't be entirely true because…
2. A more likely explanation is…
3. Another way of looking at this could be…

Let me go back to that leak in the kitchen. My initial responses were to 'catastrophise' and imagine the worst. When I had calmed down later, I could see 'another way of looking at it': *what a good job we found it now and that it didn't happen when we were on holiday, otherwise the whole house might have flooded. Luckily, it happened whilst we already had good plumbers on site, and they were able to deal with it immediately.*

This kind of self-talk is very effective for reframing a situation, helping to keep things in perspective. I have learned a lot from my husband!

Summary
A sense of perspective is undoubtedly a useful characteristic at any age. It helps to keep us grounded in reality rather than

wasting precious energy and time worrying about things which may never happen. It is even more of an advantage in later life as it seems to help people be better able to remember the past fondly but also to look ahead.

Key learnings

- A sense of perspective on life is one of the differentiators between 'super agers' and those who age less positively.
- It is possible to develop more perspective by retraining your NATs.
- Conducting a 'life review' can help people find more perspective by reframing their relationship with the past.
- The more balanced our 'whole lives' are, the better able we are to keep individual life events in perspective.
- Working with a good coach, counsellor or therapist can be a great way of developing more perspective on life.

Activities

How can we develop more perspective?

The first activity is a positive psychology technique that is also useful for developing a more optimistic outlook.

1) Permanence, Pervasiveness and Personalisation (the three P's)[2]

If something happens to you, for example getting a bad cold,

---

2   This activity is included with the kind permission of the Langley Group.

catch yourself and your automatic self-talk around this. Watch out for the following three dimensions:

- Permanence – will this last forever?
- Pervasiveness – does it affect all aspects of my life?
- Personalisation – am I to blame?

Someone who is inclined to take things out of perspective might say:

- I'm always getting sick.
- This is going to ruin all my plans.
- It's my own fault; I've not been looking after myself.

Whereas someone with a healthier sense of perspective might say:

- That's annoying, but I'm bound to feel better tomorrow.
- I can use the time to rest and catch up on my reading.
- It's likely that I caught this from my friend's daughter last week.

Can you see the difference? An optimist is better able to keep bad events in perspective, doesn't let them spoil everything or blame themselves.

Next time something bad happens, apply the three P's and actively cultivate thinking like an optimist and keeping things in perspective.

2) Forgiveness

The power of forgiveness is awesome. I would not have believed it if I had not heard all the evidence on my positive psychology programme, and I was still sceptical when we were asked to write a letter to someone we were finding it hard to forgive. I wrote two pages. When I reread it, I felt a huge sense of relief and realised I had been holding onto a lot of negative energy. Whilst I never sent the letter, the relationship with that person has shifted dramatically – I think because I let go of my grudge and moved on, allowing me to be more open to rebuilding the relationship.

Try it and see. Think of someone who has hurt you in the past and whom you are finding it difficult to forgive. This person may no longer be alive, but you could be harbouring negative emotions towards them. Write a letter of genuine forgiveness, starting with your own feelings and then trying to understand what may have been going on for them at the time. If the person is still alive and you feel it may be well received, either send the letter or, better still, go and see them in person. If not, read the letter through, tear it up and let it go. Notice how differently you feel towards them and what happens to your energy levels. Try and reframe the incident which you found hard to forgive to get it more in perspective.

3) Reverse bucket list

I like this technique of looking back on what we have achieved in our lives rather than making a long wish list of things we would like to do 'one day'.

I can vouch for the way this works. When she had Alzheimer's, my mum used to regularly bemoan the fact that she never went anywhere, especially on holiday. My sister made a list in her notebook of all the countries she had visited in her life. My dad went a step further. A keen photographer all his life, his favourite media was colour slides. So, they took regular virtual trips in the comfort of their own homes to Libya, Switzerland, Madeira, Jersey and all the places they had visited over the years. Two holidays for the price of one – remember my dad was a Yorkshireman!

Apply this to your own life. Make a list of experiences, places visited and goals already achieved. Take time to savour these and enjoy the memories. Talk to others who were involved or who are interested. Relive the experience. This may help you be more selective and realistic about what really matters most to you going forward.

Seven

Curiosity

'We keep moving forward, opening new doors and
doing new things, because we're curious and
curiosity keeps leading us down new paths.'
– Walt Disney

What is curiosity and why is it important?

Curiosity is defined as a strong desire to know or learn
something, and I believe this is one of the most important
qualities to have at any age, as it keeps us interested in others
and the world around us.

Some of the most interesting people I know are those
who are naturally inquisitive about everything and ask good
questions.

A very good friend of mine, who did not have the best
education, never stops being curious. This is how she learns,
and she would be a very good person to have in your team
for a quiz. I'm constantly amazed at the practical information
she has to hand when needed. Every year, four of us meet

up for a reunion, having shared a flat together more years ago than I care to remember. Last year we booked an Airbnb property in York, a favourite city of mine. It worked well until my friend noticed a damp patch in the living room. Two of our group could not rest until we had found the source of the leak and come up with a plan for what needed to be done about it. Two of us just carried on putting on our make-up and getting ready for our night out. I must say the landlord was very grateful for their detective work, and we were given a discounted rate for the property this year.

Curiosity is such an important character trait, not only because it widens our perspective but also because it keeps us open-minded and receptive to new experiences. Whilst we are open to these, we keep learning and wondering about the world, which stops us focusing too much on our inner world and becoming self-absorbed.

Some of the 'youngest' people I know don't define themselves by age but just keep embracing new experiences. As an elderly visitor told me recently: "I just keep saying yes to things and only reflect later whether it is possible."

There are many people, myself included, who have what I term as 'selective curiosity', which means being endlessly curious about a few favourite topics and quite closed-minded about others. In my case this means I will go the extra mile to find a new quote or piece of research on anything to do with health and well-being, yet my eyes glaze over when someone is trying to persuade me round to the benefits of the latest technology.

Whilst it is unusual to be interested in everything – candidates on *University Challenge* excepted – it is a real asset to embracing later years in a positive light. It can seem tempting for many people who are getting older to narrow their horizons and close down their options, yet it really is a time when new opportunities are available to those who look and are open-minded.

Having a growth mindset really helps here (see chapter five on adaptability), as does having a spirit of adventure, which can on occasions mean being less risk-averse and pushing out of your comfort zone. A small example of this is taking up a new sport or hobby that you haven't previously considered.

Case study

My friend Sue is passionate about penguins and has travelled extensively in pursuit of ticking off the different species from her list. Recently back from an adventure in the Antarctic, she has become a champion for the South Georgia Heritage Trust, who have done excellent work in conserving the flora, fauna and historical heritage of the islands. Sue's curiosity to learn more, combined with excitement about spreading some hope in this challenging arena, make her a powerful champion for this small charity. It has also given her a new sense of purpose.

Case study

Barbara is still a practising masseuse in her late sixties. She recently signed up for a new course on craniosacral therapy because she is fascinated by how it works. Absorbing huge amounts of theory certainly kept her brain engaged. As a natural introvert who is used to working on her own, a week in London working long days as part of a large group pushed her out of her comfort zone.

What happens if we don't have curiosity?

Something I notice in my coaching work is that when people lack curiosity, they tend to be overly focused on themselves. This can lead to low mood and lack of perspective. One of the things I enjoy most in my coaching practice is 'holding up the mirror' and reflecting back what I observe without judgement. Honest feedback is still relatively rare in British culture, and if someone is genuinely curious, it is a great way of increasing self-awareness. Some of my most valuable lightbulb moments have come from unexpected (and on occasions unwelcome) feedback which have often led to insights that have accelerated my personal growth.

As with all gifts, the best thing to say when receiving feedback is 'thank you'. It is then your choice about what to do with it. Do you value it and put it to good use straight away? Or do you tuck it into the back of your mind, either thinking it is not relevant to you or because you don't like it?

Taking on board honest and constructive feedback is one way I have learned more about myself. Yet it hasn't always come as a welcome gift, and it has sometimes taken me quite a while to accept there are common themes to several people's comments. For example, I am by nature a bit of a 'last minute Lucy', and whilst I can always meet a work deadline, it is often with very little time to spare. I can also be a few minutes late for meetings with friends or family. My long-suffering husband is just the opposite, preferring to be at the airport a good three hours before the plane leaves. We are very different personality types, and we also work together. Having been married for over forty years, I thought we had learned to accommodate and make allowances for each other's idiosyncrasies. Yet me being late and keeping him waiting was a constant source of irritation for him, and I had become immune to his impatience and complaints. As time is of less importance to me, I couldn't see why it annoyed him so much until one day he said: "I think it is rude and disrespectful to keep me waiting every time."

Goodness, what a different impact this had on me. I had never intended to be rude, and I suddenly saw it from his point of view because he expressed it in terms of values and emotions, a language I can more easily accept. Whilst I cannot say I am perfect, I do make more effort to respect his preferences, usually resulting in me putting my 'face' on at the airport but also having time for a leisurely breakfast – a 'win-win'.

Of course, people have a choice, and some people are genuinely not open or interested in other people's views. Closed-minded people tend to be quite opinionated and more focused on trying to persuade others round to their point of view. It is difficult to argue with a closed-minded person, who can be very set in their ways and believe they are right. Even more importantly, genuinely curious people are more likely to become less judgemental when they are open to different points of view.

Case study

Alice is an elderly lady in her eighties who lives on her own with the invaluable support of her daughter and daily carers. She has struggled with accepting help from them. Her daughter was getting increasingly frustrated with her mum for not letting some of the carers make her an evening meal and pushed her to find out why. She is a naturally curious person anyway and took the time to ask what the real reason behind this was without making assumptions. What emerged was Alice's fear that the carers may not all have washed their hands before touching her food. A call to the care agency and a bottle of antiseptic hand wash was all that was needed to make Alice accept help more readily.

Case study

Unfortunately, my dear dad was somewhat closed-minded. He had a certain view of the world, which he believed was right and which he tried very hard to convince others to share. When he encountered genuine curiosity, probing questions and alternative views which disputed this, he found it difficult. It made for some lively debates between him and one of my daughters, who is endlessly curious, when his views on how 'little girls' should behave were challenged when she was very young.

What does the research say?

Going back to my positive psychology learnings, I was keen to discover more when I learned that 'dialling up curiosity can dial down anxiety'. It is a muscle worth strengthening.

Sue Langley from the Langley Group talks about the following benefits experienced by curious people:

- They may be better able to handle ambiguity and uncertainty. This makes sense as, if we are keen to find out more about a forthcoming change, it can take some of the fear away.
- With regular use, curiosity contributes to exploration, discovery, growth and achievement. Quite simply, our life expands.

- Curious people are generally more open and receptive to other perspectives. They are the opposite of narrow-minded.
- Curiosity has been found to be correlated with happiness, engagement and a sense of meaning.

Todd Kashdan also adds some powerful evidence for these benefits of curiosity and more in his book *Curious? Discover the Missing Ingredient to a Fulfilling Life*.

Case study

My husband used to be very nervous about flying. He was promoted at work to a job which meant he had to look for sites for new stores across London, in a glass-bottomed helicopter! His boss sent him on a fear of flying course. Just understanding how the plane worked and what the different engine noises meant was enough to allay his fears. We have even managed to visit Australia and Japan over the last few years.

Curiosity can really help form and build relationships – if people are nervous or anxious when meeting new people, having a couple of great questions can help to diffuse any tension and lead to more engaging and friendly discussions.

This last point was reinforced for me quite profoundly when I attended an event called Life Lessons. One of the speakers was the philosopher and author Alain de Botton, who founded the School of Life. His topic was about building authentic relationships, and he invited us to turn to the person next to us and ask three very probing questions.

What a buzz and rapport was achieved by going below the safe topics of conversation – even those who already knew each other learned something new. It made me consider how rarely we talk about the things that matter.

On reflection, some of my favourite 'ice-breakers' with new people would include:

- What are you most proud of in your life?
- What fear would you most like to overcome?
- If money were no object, what would you really love to do?

> 'The important thing is not to stop questioning.
> Curiosity has its own reason for existing.'
> – Albert Einstein

How does this apply to positive ageing?

> 'A curious mind continues to grow, even as the body ages…'
> – *Irish Independent* article (2017)

Case study

Stephen Hawking is a great example of someone whose boundless scientific curiosity must have been a significant factor in keeping him alive well beyond expectations. He lived with motor neurone disease for five decades and only recently died at the age of seventy-six. He had a powerful raison d'être:

> 'My goal is simple. It is to have a complete understanding of the universe.'
> – Stephen Hawking

Case study

Jane Fonda is another good example of someone whose restless curiosity to keep learning new things has encouraged her to continually review her life goals and identity throughout eight decades.

Not only is she a fantastic role model for positive ageing (put the film *Book Club* on your list if you haven't seen it), but she genuinely seems to get a buzz out of learning.

She has always had a cause to support or fight and uses her celebrity status to raise awareness of many issues, including campaigning on Capitol Hill for action on climate change.

Her claim that she would not be buying any more new clothes was borne out by her recent appearance at the Oscars where she appeared in a dress she last wore six years ago. Unheard of on the red carpet, but this action saw her 'walking her own talk' to support sustainability.

Case study
Sir Michael Palin's quest for new adventures is well known from his travel documentaries. Now in his mid-seventies, he still makes occasional programmes which interest him. He is a good advocate for curiosity and once said:

'Of all the things, all of the human traits you should retain when you're getting older curiosity is the most important. I've always been blessed, or cursed, some may say, with an insatiable curiosity, a desire to find something out about a people and a place. That's where it all begins.'
– Sir Michael Palin

'Curiosity will conquer fear even more than bravery will.'
– James Stephens

A friend of mine was going in for a big operation. I knew she was terrified, having been through a similar operation many years ago. Her way of dealing with it was to find out all the details of what was going to be done to her and about the latest techniques. Whilst she was grateful for the fact that she could have the operation done on the NHS, she wasn't afraid to ask for a more convenient hospital and have a say in her aftercare. Common sense you might say. Unfortunately, this is not always common practice, particularly among the elderly, who all too often rely totally on the medical professionals to do the best for them. There are many people who do not seem to want to take responsibility for their own health.

How often do we say the thought of something was so much worse than the actual event? Armed with information about DVT and pulmonary embolisms, the actual aftermath of my friend's operation was better than expected. She made a much quicker recovery than she had done twenty years ago and was soon back in action.

Curiosity keeps us informed and updated about the latest developments which may affect us and can help allay our fears about ageing.

Case study

What a marvellous example David Attenborough sets for the benefits of endless curiosity – his championing the issue of climate change and biodiversity loss has had a huge impact. He has become a hero to younger generations and holds the honour of being among the most kissed waxworks in Instagram selfies at Madame Tussauds in Blackpool!

Case study
Philip Glass, a composer who is still creating new materials and performing in his eighties, demonstrates the quality of being 'relentlessly and boundlessly curious' which is so important for positive ageing.

'Studies show that a curious state of mind can help us retain information, develop empathy and establish deeper connections with others: the knock-on effects on longevity and vitality are obvious.'
*Irish Independen*t article (2017)

According to research findings by Sakaki and Murayama (*Curiosity in old age: a possible key to achieving adaptive ageing*), preserving curiosity helps older adults maintain emotional well-being. It is also protective against cognitive and physical decline due to age.

These examples provide a good incentive for us to make efforts to pursue our passions, try different things and actively cultivate curiosity in our daily lives.

Case study
I recently met up with an old colleague who, on her seventieth birthday, had set herself a challenge. Each week she decided to do three new things.

These could vary from taking a different route to a friend's house to trying something completely out of her comfort zone, such as skydiving. Whether it was coincidence or not, her eyes sparkled, and she looked years younger as she told me about some of her latest adventures. They had brought her into contact with new people and she had learned new skills, including playing the saxophone, which she had never imagined she would do.

She also continued to be curious about what was going on in others' lives and was a more interesting companion as she had entertaining stories to share.

There is some evidence to suggest that as people participate in different activities, they are training their brains to create new neural pathways. The pathways get stronger with repetition until the behaviour becomes the new normal. Another powerful example of our ability to 'rewire' our brains and influence our ageing process.

Summary

So, it seems as though developing and retaining a curious mind is a real asset to ageing more positively. There is evidence to suggest that not only does it keep people younger psychologically, but it also makes them better company to others. One of the saddest signs of ageing to me is when people become very one-way, losing interest in others and in the outside world. This is more likely to lead to isolation which is covered in more depth during the next chapter.

Key learnings

- A curious mind can be developed at any age, even when the body ages.
- Asking for feedback is a great way to learn more about yourself and can make us more aware of our 'blind spots'.
- Dialling up curiosity can dial down anxiety – the more we find out about a forthcoming change, the less fearful it is likely to seem.
- Genuinely curious people build better relationships and usually make for more interesting company.
- Curiosity helps older adults maintain emotional well-being and can protect against cognitive and physical decline.

Activities

How can we flex and develop our curiosity muscle?

Try the following activities and see how they work:

1) Seek first to understand, then to be understood (Stephen Covey)

Think of someone who has a very different viewpoint to you on an important issue – politics and religion allowed here. Tell them you are curious to learn more about why they feel the way they do. Arrange a meeting and time where you will not be interrupted. Stay in 'neutral' – agree a contract of listening actively, keeping an open mind and suspending judgemental comments. Ask open questions and listen without interrupting. Spend time listening to their beliefs, rationale and perspectives on life.

Summarise back to them what they have said in your own words (you don't have to agree) and ask if you've understood them correctly.

Thank them for their time and reflect on how being curious may have helped you understand their perspective better and whether it has influenced your own. If you are lucky, and have chosen carefully, they may be able to do the same for you. Curiosity combined with open-mindedness can really help to improve relationships.

2) Hidden treasure

Find an article in a newspaper on a topic you would usually 'pass by'. Make an effort to read, digest and process the information. Have a conversation with someone about what you learned and how this may have influenced your perspective.

3) Who's your curiosity role model?

Think of the most curious person you know. What behaviours do they demonstrate that you know you could benefit from?

- They are always looking for new experiences.

- They have a wide circle of friends from different backgrounds.
- They welcome new ideas and change.
- They ask good questions to learn more.
- They enjoy solving complicated problems or riddles.
- They often come up with better ways of doing things.

Choose one of these behaviours as a goal for yourself. Adopt a more curious mindset for a week.

Example: try something new – food, different genre of book, alternative route to work etc.

How does this feel? What did you learn? How can you become more curious?

If you want to do more work on your curiosity profile, see References and Resources.

Eight

Connectivity

'We don't have to do all this alone. We were never meant to.'
– Brené Brown

What is connectivity and why is it important?

No one is truly self-sufficient; everyone needs the company and comfort of others to thrive. Connectivity is an umbrella term for being in touch with others and is often used to describe software devices or the interconnection of transport systems.

For me, it is like a mind map of all the contacts, resources and activities which prevent me feeling alone. It encompasses many layers, such as intimate and family relationships, a circle of trusted friends, feeling part of a community, being in touch with the wider world and feeling connected to something greater than myself. My daughter describes it as a feeling of belonging.

It is the quality which stops us feeling isolated and it is no coincidence that it is included in many models which measure the quality of our well-being.

For example, Abraham Maslow, an American psychologist, created a 'hierarchy of needs' which proposes five human needs required for psychological health. Love and belonging come bang in the middle of this hierarchy of needs, and it is described as follows: 'love and belonging – friendship, intimacy, family, sense of connection'.

Social networks

Our social networks provide so much value that they are sometimes referred to as 'social capital'. This is the collective value of all the social networks in a community which offer resources we might not be able to access on our own. In other words, the sum of the parts is greater than the whole.

Once again, we can learn something from Japanese culture, which is built on social reciprocity. In Okinawa, tight-knit groups called *moais* are formed within local communities. These are informal groups of people with common interests who look out for one another – the literal meaning of *moai* is 'connected for life'. Groups of children often join a group together and go on to form lifelong friendships. Members of a *moai* contribute a set amount of money to the group, which entitles them to take part in meetings, dinners, games and common hobbies. Being part of a *moai* helps to maintain emotional and financial stability within a community, with members able to borrow funds in hard times. The feeling of belonging and support gives the individual a sense of security and helps to increase life expectancy.

In his book *Bowling Alone*, Robert Putnam describes the benefits of social capital well: 'research shows that vibrant social networks are a vital part of a healthy community and individual well-being. Social capital is also strongly linked to subjective well-being, in particular to happiness and life satisfaction'.

Whilst this is still a controversial topic, there is also some research to support the concept that social networks and social capital have both been found to decrease mortality in human population-based studies (*Social Capital and Self-Rated Health: A Contextual Analysis.* Kawachi, Kennedy and Glass).

So, the old saying 'it's not what you know but who you know' may serve us well not only for job-hunting but for living a longer and healthier life.

What happens if we don't have connectivity?

For anyone who doesn't feel a sense of connectivity, the world must seem a lonely place. We already know that loneliness is on the increase, especially for older people. According to Age UK, over half of all people over seventy-five in the UK live alone and 40% of older people say television is their main companion. Many more people were forced to spend more time alone during the 2020 Covid-19 pandemic. It was heartbreaking to hear of long-married couples being kept apart for health reasons and heartwarming to see the power of a hug on both sides with much-missed grandchildren when restrictions eased.

'Young or old, loneliness doesn't discriminate.'
– Jo Cox

Loneliness is a bigger problem than simply an emotional experience. It can be harmful to our physical and mental health. According to research, lacking social connections is as comparable a risk factor for early death as smoking fifteen cigarettes a day and is worse for us than known risk factors such as obesity and physical inactivity (Holt-Lunstad, 2017).

What does the research say?

Connectivity is a common theme among most positive psychology practitioners who observe the significant benefits in practice. As we have already identified, there are many layers to connectivity, each worthy of a more detailed section.

Connection with self

Perhaps this is the most important one. It is not until we really know and accept ourselves that we feel happy in our own company. Many people would say this needs to happen before we can build relationships with others. As someone who relishes time alone, I am sad to see people who really don't like their own company and fill their diaries just to avoid this.

Of course, there are different personality preferences, the implications of being an extrovert who prefers the company of others, or an introvert who re-energises through spending time alone, are well documented.

I'm also very grateful that I don't have to spend all my time alone and appreciate that bereavement, divorce, children leaving home and retirement are all too often the events which mean people spend time alone not always out of choice.

However, to feel truly connected to ourselves takes practice. It has taken me years to recognise my authentic feelings 'in the moment'. Yoga, meditation, journaling, affirmations and talking therapies have all been invaluable here.

I now feel more 'comfortable in my own skin' which has enabled me to act more confidently when making choices to honour my own needs most of the time and set boundaries. So, for example, I am much more likely to opt out of a group activity when I need some 'me time' without worrying what others will think.

Some people talk about connecting with their 'higher self', which I interpret as being your best self (you on a good day), and whatever it takes to access this is a worthwhile investment of time. Playing to strengths and honouring your needs are examples of strategies which will help you be your best self.

Connection with others

Positive relations with others are a key measurement of happiness and well-being on several positive psychology models.

For example, it is one of the key indicators of psychological well-being on Carol D. Ryff's Psychological Wellbeing (PWB) Scale, which we used on our DPP.

The PWB measures six aspects of well-being and happiness: autonomy, environmental mastery, personal growth, *positive relations with others*, purpose in life and self-acceptance.

This element also forms an important criterion of Martin Seligman's PERMA Model. In his book *Flourish,* he describes the elements for optimal well-being as follows:

- Positive emotions
- Engagement
- Relationships
- Meaning
- Accomplishment

Each of these five elements was covered in depth by the Langley Group on our DPP. See References and Resources for more ideas on how to develop these.

In her highly recommended book *Ten Keys to Happier Living*, Vanessa King, a board member of Action for Happiness, has coined the acronym GREAT DREAMS to help us remember all the positive practices we can do to feel happier. Several of these involve connecting with others. There is a lot of useful information on the Action for Happiness website.

Sue Langley from the Langley Group describes the importance of our relationships as critical to our overall well-being:

'If we can increase the positive influence of our
relationships, we will increase our ability to flourish.'
– Sue Langley

Thriving relationships seem to be the single most important determinant for happiness and have a powerful impact on well-being. Whilst it may sound obvious, research has found that having close friends or a romantic partner to share our experiences with can add more meaning to our lives. People with more meaningful lives report that 'relationships are more important than achievements'.

'The presence of a supportive person – or even just
thinking about them – can reduce cardiovascular
and neuroendocrine responses to stress.'
– Julianne Holt-Lunstad

Research from positive psychology also shows that positive emotions make people more sociable and willing to cultivate relationships. Good relationships are associated with better physical and mental health. Happier people have stronger friendships and romantic relationships and are also more likely to volunteer.

Dr. Chris Peterson, one of the founders of positive psychology, put it succinctly – 'other people matter'.

The power of strengths
A good place to start building better relationships is by

noticing and validating one another's strengths. As a coach, I have noticed how hard people can be on themselves. In the UK, in my experience, it is also rare to find an organisation where praise is a regular part of the culture. Many people can easily list five 'weaknesses' but squirm in their seats if I ask them for their top five strengths. So, it can be useful to find a way of highlighting these. Giving and receiving feedback is one way of doing this. The best self activity at the end of chapter two on optimism is a good place to start.

Strength spotting in others can also become a very useful skill in building connections and developing relationships. This relies on you actively listening out for the innate strengths people have which they may not be aware of or take for granted. See the end of this chapter for more details on this activity.

Cappfinity is the global leader in strengths-based assessments, and I can highly recommend their strengths profiles for learning more about what you are good at and, even more importantly, what strengths energise you. They have just introduced a free introductory profile.

A word about pets

Of course, connection with A.N. Other doesn't necessarily have to be with a person. Many people who would otherwise be lonely get a great deal of comfort from their pets. Dogs, for example, can provide unconditional love and are often called 'man's best friend'.

Case study

George was widowed after losing his wife following a long illness. He was devastated and, without a family, felt lost on his own. However, his wife had left him a companion: her little Scottie dog called Clyde. While she was alive, George had never had much time for the dog, but he gradually started to enjoy his company, recalling funny incidents and happy memories which enabled him to feel some connection with his wife. There is no doubt that caring for Clyde and taking regular walks provided a structure to George's day when he needed it most.

Social interaction

What is the communication like in your relationships? In our positive psychology group we all had the idea that being there for someone when they were having a difficult time was something which reinforced a stronger relationship. Yet, we were surprised to find that it was even more important to celebrate good events together. C.A. Langston (1994) termed the phrase 'capitalisation' – the very act of sharing good news magnifies its impact, giving additional benefit to the experience. This could be one explanation why Instagram has become so popular. It was also poignantly reinforced by TV presenter Kate Garraway recently when she said what she missed most about her husband Derek Draper being in hospital was 'sharing funny stories about the kids'.

Most people are well aware of the impact a positive and negative relationship can have on us. However, it was interesting to learn that John Gottman, the American psychological researcher who did extensive research on divorce prediction and marital stability, suggests that the ratio of positive to negative interactions should ideally exceed 5:1 for a relationship to flourish. I'm guessing that leaves room for improvement in most relationships!

Connecting with community

'Alone we can do so little, together we can do so much.'
– Helen Keller

This is an important connection, and research found that more than 83% of people over seventy feel they belong to their neighbourhood (Office for National Statistics).

Case study
Having lived in our small community for over thirty years, I have seen many people move in and out of our road. Most of us were on nodding terms with our neighbours but little more. It took some new blood on the Residents Association Committee to set up a Residents WhatsApp Group and encourage us to be truly neighbourly. We now have a welcome pack for new residents with useful local resources and contact

details. People have a much easier way of checking in on each other, sharing helpful information and promoting social events. I am only sorry that it took us so long to develop this community spirit.

Of course, there are pockets of loneliness within all age groups and not just among older people.

'In our age-segregated society – some people simply don't know any old people.'
– Professor Molly Andrews

Even though there are more ways than ever to be 'connected', there is a sense of isolation amongst many young people today. Outside of the workplace there are some good intergenerational initiatives which are making a real difference. A few examples include:

- Age UK offer a befriending service, which links up a volunteer befriender with an older person for a chat or a visit. Become a Dementia Friend is also a good initiative from the Alzheimer's Society. This involves helping people live with dementia and raising awareness. Volunteers from both initiatives report a real feel-good factor.
- Homeshare UK matches people with spare rooms with people who are happy to provide company and

lend a hand around the house in return for affordable accommodation and mutual companionship. All candidates are carefully vetted, and the scheme allows elderly people to remain independent in their own homes for longer, whilst providing affordable accommodation to those who need it at a time of record housing shortages and high rents.

- Intergenerational care, e.g. Apples and Honey Nightingale, a nursery set up within Nightingale House, a Jewish care home in South London. Benefits to both age groups have been significant (*How care homes and nurseries are coming together for good*. Age UK. April 2018).

- North London Cares is a community network which puts young professionals in touch with older people within some London boroughs. As communities transform, many older people who have lived in the city all their lives can feel left behind and 'disconnected' as the pace of life increases. Young professionals moving into London may be digitally well connected but have few real contacts with people. By bringing people together, North London Cares aims to reduce loneliness and improve connection between the generations.

- Paul Sinton Hewitt CBE FRSA founded Park Run, an all-inclusive 5k Saturday morning event run nationwide and open to all ages. Entry is free – it is run by volunteers, and there is no time limit. Whole families can take part and it has now spread to over two thousand locations across twenty-two countries. Having both participated and volunteered at Park Run, I can vouch for the community spirit and feel-good factor this provides.

Volunteering

When we give of ourselves, life gives back. Many people report feeling more fulfilled, connected and with a greater sense of purpose.

> 'Every super ager I've come across volunteers.'
> – Max Pemberton

Case study

I have an elderly friend who organises a group called 'Time for Tea' which meets monthly and usually in someone's house. They choose speakers who live in interesting locations to host the events. My husband and I agreed to do a talk on Japan after a holiday there. The group duly arrived, complete with volunteer carers for the infirm and their own afternoon tea and crockery. We had totally underestimated the genuine enthusiasm and curiosity of the group. For some, it was their only outing of the month, and they were delighted to catch up with each other. They also asked so many questions that we ran out of time but promised a rerun some time – a good excuse for choosing another exotic holiday location. What was also interesting was that it was hard to differentiate some of the 'carers' from members of the group in terms of age. Volunteering certainly helped them feel good and think of themselves as younger.

One study found that volunteering tended to increase healthy lifespan as long as the volunteer's motives were to help others rather than for their own personal satisfaction (*Wisconsin Longitudinal Study*). Some of the health benefits included staying active and reduced depression among consistent volunteers. Other fringe benefits noted in regular volunteers seem to include taking your mind off your own troubles, meeting new people, as well as feeling good about doing something worthwhile.

Mentoring also seems to provide a similar feel-good factor to volunteering – indeed it is often an unpaid activity, which can work well between different generations. This is a good way of passing on skills and knowledge which seems to have as many benefits for the mentor (staying in touch, giving something back, helping others) as the mentee (learning new skills, considering different perspectives, having an objective supporter).

In my own life and career, I have been lucky enough to have had some brilliant mentors who sometimes believed in me more than I did myself at the time. I now get great pleasure in mentoring others and passing on some of my own learning.

Case study

Along with many others, I was incredibly moved by the efforts of Captain Sir Tom Moore, a war veteran, who raised over £32 million for NHS charities during the 2020 Covid-19 pandemic. His initial goal was to raise £1,000 by completing one hundred circuits of his garden before his one hundredth birthday. What a powerful example he set of being motivated by a greater cause. He became quite a celebrity in his last few months, receiving more than 150,000 birthday cards and being given a knighthood. He will be remembered as someone who inspired the nation with his positive approach to life and his saying that 'tomorrow will be a good day'.

Global connections

Social networks and friendships not only have an impact on reducing the risk of mortality or developing certain diseases, but they also help individuals to recover when they do fall ill (Marmot, 2010).

So, there is a huge incentive to encourage everyone to stay connected, whether to friends and family, the wider community or more globally through social media or the internet. Despite the bad press about social media, it can be an invaluable source of company and helps people feel connected, especially when friends and family live abroad.

No wonder the 'silver surfers' are increasing in number.

I am especially grateful to WhatsApp, Facetime and Voice Notes for helping me stay in touch with my daughter when she spent a year living abroad in a very different time zone. This kind of connection was not available to my parents' generation, who had to suffice with an odd postcard when I was on my own travels as a teenager.

'Almost a third of internet users over 65 say email and/or social media is their main means of keeping in touch with extended family.'
– Nelson Research, 2015

'Smartphone ownership is now growing most rapidly for the over 75s.'
– OFCAM, 2018

Case study

Picking up the phone for a chat is increasingly rare but can often be a lifeline to older people. I have an aunt, now in her late eighties, who lives on her own. She has a mischievous sense of humour, and we have several things in common, often sending silly poems to each other. I get just as much out of our occasional telephone conversations as I hope she does.

Case study

Kate is an energetic, vivacious woman in her seventies. A grandma to seven, several of her grandchildren live far away, some in New Zealand and others in Los Angeles. She has become very resourceful at keeping in touch and now has her own YouTube channel where she posts regular video clips of herself baking, dancing, being a DJ at a friend's party etc. She's a popular granny!

I do sometimes wonder what we all did without mobile phones and Google. While writing this book, I have become very reliant on checking out research this way, and my daily screen time has doubled. I have had to be quite disciplined with my 'digital detox' times to maintain my focus. I work for myself, so in theory it should be easy, but there is an addictive pull encouraged by social media sites, which requires real personal discipline to resist. We owe it to ourselves to develop healthier habits which make technology work for us and increase rather than decrease our well-being.

Connection with something 'bigger'

This feeling of being part of something greater than oneself can be manifested in different ways. It might be being part of a community, a cause, a sports team, a faith, movement or religion. The way the nation comes together during Wimbledon or football championships is a great example of connectivity.

Being a member of Action for Happiness is something which fulfils that need in me. I always come away from meetings and events feeling uplifted, knowing that we are part of a global movement for the greater good. They run regular live global events with expert speakers and offer free digital coaching based on their 10 Keys to Happier Living available to everyone. Altruism at its best.

There is also a sense of legacy involved, feeling part of something bigger and giving back, as this Greek proverb illustrates so well:

> 'A society grows great when old people plant
> trees under whose shade they will never sit.'
> – Greek Proverb

Spending time in nature is another great way of connecting with both your inner self and something far greater. Just going for a short walk in the fresh air can be enough to lift your mood and give you an appreciation of the beauty of the natural world. I always come away feeling more 'grounded' and positive after even a short walk.

How does this apply to positive ageing?
Staying connected undoubtedly has a big impact on the way people age. We have already seen the downsides of loneliness and it is in our interests to be proactive when it comes to keeping up with our friends, contacts and families, wherever they might be in the world.

Case study

An elderly friend of mine lives alone. Yet you wouldn't know it. Whenever I have popped round for a cup of tea, there has always been someone calling round or ringing up. She often has people to stay, which she loves. And yet, she has no family. As a volunteer on several committees, she has quite simply built her own community around her and befriended people of all ages. Nearly ninety, she regularly attends funerals, yet these are offset by the company of young people who she has befriended and on occasions given a home to. She uses her iPad to keep in touch with the world and is determined to keep her independence for as long as she can. She told me that she would hate to have to go into a care home where she might only be with people her own age. I feel privileged to be called one of her younger friends.

Connectivity and kindness

One of the most interesting pieces of research I heard recently was on the benefits of kindness. It seems that this can literally rewire our brains to age more slowly.

Dr. David R. Hamilton, compassion expert and author of *The Little Book of Kindness*, was a speaker at Life Lessons. He positioned kindness as the antidote to stress and provided evidence that practising kindness can effect changes in the brain which slow down the ageing process.

By practising the loving kindness meditation for six weeks, a group of people actively changed the neuroplasticity of their brain and slowed down the rate of shortening of their telomeres. Short telomeres, the little end caps on our DNA that stop it unravelling, mean faster ageing.

Kindness can slow down the ageing process, and other side effects include:

- Happiness increases as brain chemistry actually changes.
- Relationships improve.
- Kindness is contagious.
- It's good for the heart both literally and metaphorically.

So, what are we waiting for? The loving kindness meditation, which we experienced first-hand on our DPP, is described in more detail in the activities at the end of this chapter.

Summary

Connectivity is one of the most important qualities we can develop as we get older. It widens our horizons, keeps us up to date, brings the benefits of social interaction and can prevent loneliness and depression.

Key learnings

- Thriving relationships seem to be the single most important determinant for happiness and well-being.
- Sharing good news improves intimate relationships

more than being supported through difficult times.

- People who volunteer consistently live significantly longer than those who don't.
- Practising kindness to self and others as a regular habit has been proven to slow down the ageing process.

Activities

How to feel more connected

Here are three suggestions about how you might improve your sense of connection:

1) Strengths spotting

Choose someone who you already know quite well but with whom you want to develop a better relationship. This may be a partner, a friend or work colleague. Tell them you are doing some personal development and need to practise your listening skills. Let them know you will be taking notes. Ask them to share a story of one of their proudest moments, when they felt they had done something well. Some people find this hard, so give them time to think about this. Your job is to listen, affirm non-verbally, e.g. smile, nod, encourage them to say more. At the end of their story, let them know what strengths you heard them describe when they were at their best and notice their reaction. Ask if they will do the same for you.

This is a great activity to do as a family, on a regular basis. It can also be particularly mood-boosting for older people who can be very hard on themselves.

2) Loving kindness meditation[3]

This meditation is widely practised in positive psychology as 'compassion meditation'. According to David R. Hamilton, practising this daily will keep you physiologically younger.

Step one: choose a quiet place. Close your eyes and breathe deeply five times. Say these words out loud three times: *may I be filled with loving kindness, be well, at ease, happy and free from suffering.* Pause and reflect.

Step two: then apply the same phrase but instead of 'I' insert the name of a loved one. Say this out loud three times. Pause and reflect.

Step three: then apply the same phrase but insert the name of someone you dislike or have a negative emotion towards. This might be harder to do but again repeat the phrase out loud three times. Pause and reflect – do you feel differently towards them?

Practise this every day if you can for six weeks and note the difference. The power of forgiveness not only has beneficial effects on relationships but also on your health, in particular blood pressure readings and stress levels.

3) Making new connections

What cause/issues/injustices do you feel so strongly about that you would go out on a limb to change?

---

3   Reproduced by kind permission of the Langley Group

Examples: the stigma around mental health, the assumption that we cannot influence our own ageing process.

Make a note of one or two of your own which come to mind. How could you make a difference? Financially or using your time, experience and strengths? Who do you know who might know more about these topics? How can you connect with them? Make a note of when you will do this.

This should give you a genuine reason for getting in touch with people to 'pick their brains' on a subject they know more about than you. This activity may also help you clarify your sense of purpose and develop your 'curiosity muscle'.

Personal Action Plan

So, we come almost to the end of the book. You have read about each of the eight traits which can help you flourish in later life. You may even have completed some of the activities at the end of each chapter.

Now it is time to translate all your good intentions into action. This section of the book can be used to reinforce your positive mindset and intentions to make the most of the next phase of your life.

There are three things to do next:

1) Compete this short questionnaire on the eight characteristics of positive agers:

Ageing Rewired – how will you 'flourish' in later life?		
Please consider yourself against the following traits and give yourself a score from 1 – 5 (1 being low, 5 being high). A few tips: we are often harder on ourselves than others would be so try not to overthink your responses or worry about 'blowing your own trumpet'. If you know you are having a bad day, revisit it when you have a different perspective.		
Trait	**Description**	**Score**
Sense of purpose (*ikigai*)	Feel that I have a worthwhile and meaningful contribution to make, a 'raison d'être', which motivates me each day.	
Optimism	Have a 'can do' approach, expect the best and actively work on developing a positive mental attitude. Count my blessings, practise gratitude, have a strong belief system.	
Resilience	Learn from the past and 'bounce beyond' setbacks, overcome adversity. Know how to keep myself in a good place and invest time, energy and resources in doing so.	
Proactivity	Take responsibility, anticipate change and take action. Feel autonomous and confident to be 'my own person'.	
Adaptability	Accept and embrace change, let go of out-of-date thoughts and behaviours. Able to control mixed emotions and adjust to new circumstances.	
Perspective	Don't sweat the small stuff; look at life as a whole and able to keep things in balance. Can identify what's within my control and what's not. Don't take life too seriously.	
Curiosity	Interested in other people, the world generally and keen to keep learning new things. Open minded and tolerant of differences. Don't define myself by age.	
Connectivity	Have a good social circle and support networks. Feel part of a community and often volunteer time or resources. Actively stay in touch with others.	

2) Scoring and next steps

a) Transfer your scores onto the pie chart below

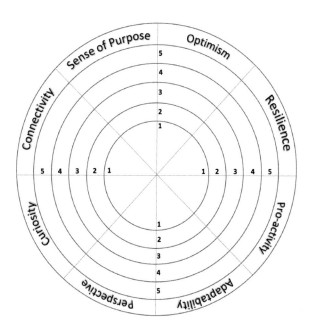

b) Note your highest scores and give yourself a pat on the back – these are your strengths so do more of them as they serve you well.

3) Personal action plan

c) Now pick out two or three of your lower scores – decide which areas you want to work on to further develop these characteristics.

d) Make a note of at least three key actions you can take to increase your chances of flourishing in later life.

Personal example – here is my own completed pie chart:

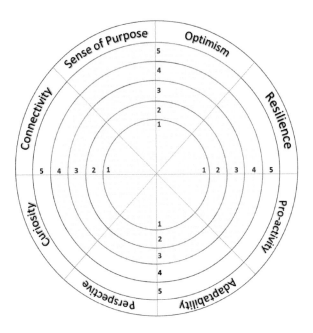

My lowest scores are in adaptability and perspective, and my three key actions are as follows:

1. Keep working on accepting all my mixed emotions around times of change; use the Four A's technique and journaling to help me process these (see chapter three on resilience).

2. Notice my overreactions to certain events – remember the thinking traps and my tendency to 'catastrophise'. Challenge these thoughts by using the phrase 'another way of looking at this might be…' or the three P's (see chapter six on perspective).

3. Continue to talk to those who have a different perspective on life and who can help me reframe my thinking.

Maintaining momentum

Be patient with yourself and practise your own actions daily. It takes twenty-one days to break an old habit and sixty-six days to reinforce a new one. You may like to 'buddy up' with someone and encourage each other.

Retake the Ageing Rewired Questionnaire after three months of practising new techniques from the book and celebrate your progress. Review which areas you still want to work on. This action plan is a work in progress; the main person who will benefit is *you* but there may also be a 'positive ripple' effect on others. Something else you may wish to revisit now you are more informed is the Purpose Triangle from chapter one. See next page and refer to P19 for guidelines.

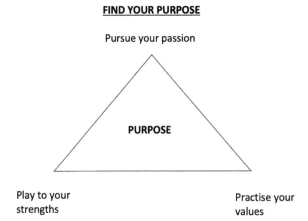

FIND YOUR PURPOSE

Pursue your passion

PURPOSE

Play to your
strengths

Practise your
values

A final word

Congratulations! The act of reading this book has already set you on the right path for flourishing in later life. To continue your journey of self-development, dip into the References and Resources section for further ideas and reading.

Remember to celebrate your achievements along the way. I'd love to hear some of your stories and experiences of using the book, so if you'd like to get in touch, please contact me on the email address below:

lynne@lbdassociates.co.uk

I wish you well!

References and Resources

Chapter One – Sense of Purpose

P2 *Nothing Like a Dame* documentary: https://www.justwatch.com/uk/movie/nothing-like-a-dame

P3 *Ikigai – The Japanese Secret to a Long and Happy Life.* Hector Garcia and Francesc Miralles

P4 Diploma of positive psychology and wellbeing – Langley Group: https://langleygroupinstitute.com/diploma-of-positve-psychology-and-wellbeing/

P5 Strengths profiles – Cappfinity: https://www.strengthsprofile.com/

P6 Action for Happiness website and access to free app: https://www.actionforhappiness.org/smartphone-app

P8 Life balance – See appendix 1

P9 *Counterclockwise – A Proven Way to Think Yourself Younger and Healthier.* Ellen J. Langer

P9 *Your Time to Thrive – End Burnout, Increase Well-being, and Unlock Your Full Potential with the New Science of Microsteps.* Arianna Huffington

P9 *Man's Search for Meaning* – Viktor E. Frankl

P11 *The Human Quest for Meaning.* Paul T.P.Wong

P12 *Your Body Speaks Your Mind.* Deb Shapiro

P12 *You Can Heal Your Life.* Louise Hay

P12 Craniosacral therapy (CST): https://www.craniosacral.co.uk/

P13 Psychological wellbeing (PWB) questionnaire. Carol Ryff. Contact Carol Ryff directly at cryff@wisc.edu

P13 *The State of Ageing in 2019.* Centre for Ageing Better: https://www.ageing-better.org.uk

P15 Via Strengths – website and survey: https://www.viacharacter.org

Chapter Two – Optimism

P21 *A Short Course in Happiness After Loss: and Other Dark Difficult Times.* Maria Sirois

P25 *The State of Ageing in 2019.* Centre for Ageing Better: https://www.ageing-better.org.uk

P25 American Association of Retired Persons (AARP): https://www.aarp.org/

P26 *The How of Happiness.* Sonja Lyubomirsky

P28 *Learned Optimism.* Martin Seligman

P31 *Broaden-and-Build Theory of Positive Emotions.* Nicole Celestine: https://positivepsychology.com/broaden-build-theory/

Chapter Three – Resilience

Chapter Four – Proactivity

P61 Self-determination theory (SDT) – check out these websites for information on this and so many more positive psychology strategies: https://members.learnwithsue.com.au/podcasts/. Self-Determination Theory of Motivation: Why Intrinsic Motivation Matters (positivepsychology.com)

P63 *The Age Well Plan*. Susan Saunders

P63 *Body Wise*. Dr. Rachel Carlton Abrams

P63 *How Your Mind Can Heal Your Body*. David R. Hamilton, PhD

Chapter Five – Adaptability

P72 *This Too Shall Pass*. Julia Samuels

P82 *Mindset: The New Psychology of Success*. Carol S. Dweck, PhD

P82 Cognitive behavioural therapy (CBT): https://www.nhs.uk/mental-health/talking-therapies-medicine-treatments/talking-therapies-and-counselling/cognitive-behavioural-therapy-cbt/overview/

P84 Unclaimed Conversation Cards. Liminal Space: https://shop.barbican.org.uk/products/unclaimed-conversation-cards

Chapter Six – Perspective

P92 Myers-Briggs Type Indicator (MBTI): https://www.myersbriggs.org/my-mbti-personality-type/mbti-basics/. Or try this website for a free version of this: https://www.16personalities.com/

P94 *Feel the Fear and Do It Anyway*. Susan Jeffers

P96 *The State of Ageing in 2019*. Centre for Ageing Better

P97 *Bolder – Life lessons from people older and wiser than you*. Dominique Afacan and Helen Cathcart

P97 TED Talk – Life's Third Act. Jane Fonda: https://www.ted.com/talks/jane_fonda_life_s_third_act?language=en

P97 *How to Age Positively*. Guy Robertson

P99 *Change Your Life with CBT*. Corinne Sweet

P101 Positive psychology masterclass. Bridget Grenville-Cleave and Miriam Akhtar: https://www.workmad.co.uk/positive-psychology-masterclass/

Chapter Seven – Curiosity

P108 South Georgia Heritage Trust (SGHT): https://www.sght.org/

P113 *Curious? Discover the Missing Ingredient to a Fulfilling Life*. Todd Kashdan

P114 The School of Life: https://www.theschooloflife.com/

P122 Further work on curiosity: https://hbr.org/2015/12/assessment-whats-your-curiosity-profile

P122 *How to Increase Your Curiosity for a Better Self*. Laura Winter: https://medium.com/the-winter-writer/how-to-increase-your-curiosity-for-a-better-self-a861f921f7fc

Chapter Eight – Connectivity

P124 *A Theory of Human Motivation*. Abraham H. Maslow

P125 *Bowling Alone*. Robert Putnam

P127 Playing to Strengths: https://www.viacharacter.org/topics/articles/how-character-strengths-help%20us-through-trying-times

P127 Psychological wellbeing (PWB) questionnaire. Carol Ryff Contact Carol Ryff directly at cryff@wisc.edu

P128 *Flourish*. Martin Seligman

P128 PERMA Model. Martin Seligman: https://ppc.sas.upenn.edu/learn-more/perma-theory-well-being-and-perma-workshops

P128 *Ten Keys to Happier Living*. Vanessa King: https://www.actionforhappiness.org/10-keys

P130 Cappfinity strengths profiles: https://www.cappfinity.com/strengths-profile/

P133 Age UK befriending service: https://www.ageuk.org.uk/services/befriending-services/

P133 Become a Dementia Friend: https://www.dementiafriends.org.uk/

P133 Homeshare UK: https://homeshareuk.org/

P134 North London Cares: https://northlondoncares.org.uk/home

P134 Park Run: https://www.parkrun.org.uk/

P140 Action for Happiness Events: https://www.actionforhappiness.org/events

P141 *The Little Book of Kindness*. Dr. David Hamilton

Further Reading

Other books which have influenced my thinking on this topic:

Live Your Dash – Make Every Moment Matter. Linda Ellis

When I am an Old Woman I Shall Wear Purple. Jenny Joseph

Extra Time – 10 Lessons for an Ageing World. Camilla Cavendish

The 100-Year Life – Living and Working in an Age of Longevity.
Lynda Gratton & Andrew Scott

The 10 Secrets of Healthy Ageing.
Patrick Holford and Jerome Burne

The Age of Ageing Better – A Manifesto for our Future.
Dr. Anna Dixon

When We're 64 – Your Guide to a Great Later Life.
Louise Ansari

*The Book About Getting Older: For People Who Don't Want to
Talk About It.* Dr. Lucy Pollock

The Tick of Two Clocks – A Tale of Moving On. Joan Bakewell

*The Strengths Profile Book – Finding What You Can Do +
Love to Do And Why It Matters.*
Alex Linley and Trudy Bateman (from Cappfinity)

Appendices:

Appendix 1 – What shape is your life?

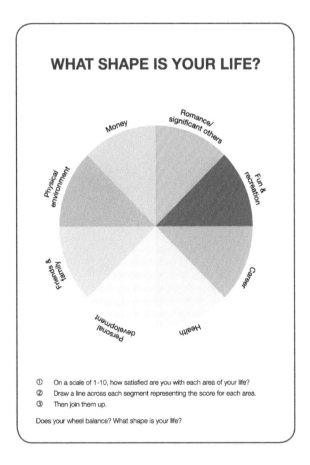

WHAT SHAPE IS YOUR LIFE?

- Money
- Romance/ significant others
- Fun & recreation
- Physical environment
- Career
- Friends & family
- Health
- Personal development

① On a scale of 1-10, how satisfied are you with each area of your life?
② Draw a line across each segment representing the score for each area.
③ Then join them up.

Does your wheel balance? What shape is your life?

Appendix 2 – What can we put in our 40% Bucket?

Brain	Body
<ul><li>Meditation / mindfulness</li><li>Practise gratitude</li><li>Keep a journal</li><li>Positive self-talk</li><li>Visualisation</li><li>Write down your goals</li><li>Learn something new</li><li>Play to your strengths</li></ul>	<ul><li>Drink lemon water</li><li>Good nutrition</li><li>Laugh daily</li><li>Enjoy new clothes</li><li>Optimise your sleep</li><li>Pamper yourself</li><li>Breathe deeply</li><li>Exercise and stretch daily</li></ul>
Environmental	**Relationships**
<ul><li>Take a holiday</li><li>Switch off screens</li><li>Get outside in nature</li><li>Visit somewhere new</li><li>Put on some music</li><li>Get up and move</li><li>Read a good book</li><li>Get organised</li></ul>	<ul><li>Connect with people daily</li><li>Send cards / letters to 'old friends'</li><li>Celebrate and share success</li><li>Appreciation – affirm the positives</li><li>Practise Random Acts of Kindness</li><li>Volunteer for a favourite cause</li><li>Enjoy time with pets</li><li>Talk things through with someone</li></ul>

Acknowledgements

This book would never have happened without the input, ideas and support from so many people. My heartfelt appreciation goes to you all.

Firstly, to the 'book midwives' – Erika, for inspiring me to stop talking and start writing and her unwavering confidence that I could actually pull this off; Corinne and Bridget, fellow authors who passed on tips and believed in me even when the going got tough; Barbara and John for their practical support and editing to help me get this over the finishing line.

I'm also indebted to my focus groups for sharing experiences and useful tips, some of my coaching clients, friends and family for agreeing to provide case studies and stories to enrich the narrative. For obvious reasons, some wish to remain anonymous, but you know who you are. Thank you.

To several other writers and researchers for allowing me to quote some of their findings, in particular to Sue Langley for sparking my interest in the topic and generously sharing some of her positive psychology models.

And finally, to my family – my husband Brian for his endless patience, technical assistance and faith in me; Vicki for her encouragement, enthusiasm and occasional pep talks; and Joanna, for her editing skills, creative input and her special blend of support and challenge along the way.

I'm not sure I could have done this without you all. Thank you.